# Stop the Copying with Wild and Wacky Research Projects

# Stop the Copying with Wild and Wacky Research Projects

**Nancy Polette**

## Teacher Ideas Press

An imprint of Libraries Unlimited
Westport, Connecticut • London

**Library of Congress Cataloging-in-Publication Data**

Polette, Nancy.
    Stop the copying with wild and wacky research projects / Nancy Polette.
      p. cm.
    Includes bibliographical references and index.
    ISBN 978-1-59158-696-8 (alk. paper)
    1. Creative teaching. 2. Creative thinking—Research. 3. Creative writing. I. Title.
  LB1025.3.P644    2008
  371.3'0281—dc22         2007050096

British Library Cataloguing in Publication Data is available.

Library of Congress Catalog Card Number: 2007050096
ISBN: 978-1-59158-696-8

First published in 2008

Libraries Unlimited, 88 Post Road West, Westport, CT 06881
A Member of the Greenwood Publishing Group, Inc.
www.lu.com

Printed in the United States of America

The paper used in this book complies with the
Permanent Paper Standard issued by the National
Information Standards Organization (Z39.48–1984).

10  9  8  7  6  5  4  3  2  1

# Contents

**Part Seven: Unbelievable People**

**Part Eight: Bits of History**

**Part Eight: Bits of History (*Cont.*)**

**Part Nine: The Earth and Its Creatures**

**Part Ten: The Unexplained**

# Preface

Did you know . . .

A famous French chef created her greatest recipe BEFORE she learned to cook!

McDonald's opened its first restaurant as a barbecue stand.

The first airmail letters went by train.

The top speed of the first automobile was three miles per hour.

A young man with no medical training served as a resident doctor in a major hospital.

The best way to prevent a toothache is to wear a dead mole around your neck.

The best way to get rid of a dead whale is to blow it up with dynamite.

These and many other wild and wacky (BUT TRUE) tales serve as springboards to research about people, places, animals, and events. In place of the traditional research report, students create songs, poems, quizzes, games, and a host of other products while at the same time meeting national standards in reading, language arts, and information literacy. **The research reporting models are generic in that they can be used to report on any person, animal, place, or event.**

*Stop the Copying with Wild and Wacky Research Projects* gives students the opportunity to explore the strange, the unusual, and the out-of-the-ordinary found on this wonderful planet we all share and to display understanding of a topic by creating unique research products in which they can take pride.

## RESEARCH HAS NEVER BEEN THIS MUCH FUN!

## Introduction

By the time students have reached the third grade, copying is fairly pervasive when research reports are assigned. Telling students not to copy but to put the information "in your own words" is another way of asking students to take something that is written well and write it poorly.

Many research models encourage copying by leaving out an important step. Examine this basic research model:

1. Select a topic

2. Survey and narrow the topic

3. Develop questions

4. Locate resources

5. Take notes

6. Organize the information

7. Share the information

The missing, and most important, step is to determine the research product upon which all other steps depend. This should be step 2. For example, in a study of ancient Egypt, if the research product is a scale model of a pyramid, the questions and resources used will be very different from the information required if the product is a one-week diary of an Egyptian slave.

The sample research reporting activity on page xi uses wild and wacky stories to stimulate interest in a topic. It then allows students to examine and select a research reporting model with which they are comfortable (which prevents copying).

To introduce the practice of doing research without copying to younger students, or to break the copying habits of older students, it is essential that information be organized and reported in new ways. The mark of a literate person is the ability to encode information in a variety of ways. *Wild and Wacky Research* provides more than 50 research reporting models that prevent copying and result in original products in which students can take pride.

The following models are generic; they can be used to report on any topic:

- Fact or Myth? (p. 6). A statement about the topic is given on one page, asking the reader whether the statement is fact or myth. The answer, along with supporting data, is given on the next page.

- Cinquain (p. 23) or diamante (p. 38). These short poetry models are used to describe a person, place, or animal.

- Ten Reasons (p. 28). This model requires the student to analyze a topic in depth to come up with 10 reasons NOT to do something, for example, 10 reasons not to visit a castle, 10 reasons not to have an alligator for a pet.

- Acrostic (p. 85). The topic is described in short sentences or phrases, with each line beginning with a letter of the topic name.

- A–Z Report (p. 74). A variation on the acrostic. The topic is presented in 26 phrases or sentences, with each phrase or sentence beginning with a letter of the alphabet.

- Newspaper. The topic is described as news, as advertisements, as an editorial, as want ads, or as other parts of a newspaper.

# HOW TO STOP COPYING USING WILD AND WACKY RESEARCH

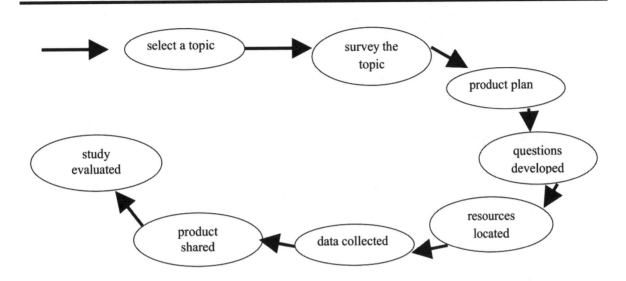

**Share:** Motivate students to research food by sharing several of the wild and wacky (but true) food tales. Example: tales about the onion and the potato chip.

**Select a Topic:** Examine and choose a food (e.g., orange).

**Choose a Product Model:** I will write an "Ode to an Orange," which contains a description, source, contents, nutritional properties, and value to and uses by humans.

**Develop Questions:** What is the source? What are the various layers of an orange? Which parts are edible? What are the nutritional values? How are oranges used by humans?

**Determine Resources:** *Where Does Food Come From?* by Shelley Rotner (Millbrook Press, 2006); *Eating Right* by Helen Frost (Pebble Books, 2000).

**Collect and Organize Data:** Gather data to answer the questions and arrange the information following the "Ode to an Onion" model (page 4).

**Share the Product** with others.

**Evaluate:** Does the "Ode" contain all needed information? Could any part of the research process have been done more efficiently?

### Ode to an Orange

I am an orange.
From fragrant blossom to a fully rounded fruit I am plucked from a tree.
My leathery rind hides the delicate flesh beneath.
My greatest need is to guard my vitamin C, which fights the common cold.
My vitamin A keeps eyesight sharp and keen.
My job is to strengthen the immune system of humans.
My former home, the tree, will continue to produce my cousins for 50 to 80 years.
I vacation when 40 percent of me is turned into juice.
My greatest desire is to bring joy to a child by being found in a Christmas stocking.
I am an orange!

# BIOGRAPHY REPORTS

- Share several of the wild and wacky stories about people. Allow time for students to respond to the stories.

- Introduce one or more of the following models. Note the information called for in each model. Allow students to choose the model they want to use in reporting research on either an assigned person or a person of their choice.

 Flight Bag/Suitcase (p. 18): What would the contents tell about a person?

 Song/Ballad (p. 26): Use a familiar tune to relate an important incident in the person's life.

 Simile Report (p. 21): Compare life events. For example, Bessie's family was as poor as an empty piggy bank.

 Who, What, When, Where, Why Report (p. 48).

 Song Connections (p. 58): Connect a famous person with various song titles and explain the connection using events in the person's life.

 Paul Revere Poetry: Summarize the person's life or retell an important incident in rhyming verse, with two to three words per line.

 Metaphor Report: Use metaphors to describe the person and explain the choices of metaphor. For example, Davy Crockett was a rock. Despite the danger he faced, he refused to move and remained steadfast at the Alamo, resulting in his death.

 Limerick: Using the limerick form of verse, give one or two facts about the person.

 Rap: Use a rap form to review a person's life or an important incident in his or her life.

 Obituary: Write an obituary and design an appropriate headstone for the person.

 Bio Poem: Report information about the person using these prompts:

**Example:**

**Charlotte Parkhurst**

**I am** a stagecoach driver

**I wonder** if I can keep my secret forever

**I hear** the pounding of horses' hooves in my sleep

**I see** trough and winding trails

**I want** to deliver my passengers safely

**I pretend** I am a man

**I touch** the reins with experienced hands

**I cry** never, showing no weakness

**I say** a woman can do any job a man can do

**I try** to avoid robbers but

**I give** as good as I get.

**I am** Charlotte Parkhurst

# REPORTING ON PLACES AND EVENTS

Share several of the stories from Part Eight, "Bits of History"; Part Nine, "The Earth and Its Creatures"; or Part Ten, "The Unexplained."

Assign, or allow students to choose, a place or an event from history to research.

Introduce one or more of the following models for reporting the research:

Cause/Effect Model (p. 88): Describe an event by giving six reasons why it happened.

Disaster Model: Beware, beware of the (disaster) there! Describe the event in six to eight sentences. Repeat the first line.

Step-by-Step Model (p. 82): Describe the steps in a process or historical events in the order in which they happened, then give an alternative outcome.

**Example:**

    **I wonder why they . . .**

Prepare the soil

Plant the seeds

Cultivate the earth

Spray the crops

Pick the cotton

Remove the fibers

Bale the lint

Truck the bales

Clean the cotton

Spin the thread

Weave the yarn

Dye the cloth

Cut and sew

When I could wear

WOOL INSTEAD!

BioEvent (p. 102): Report on a historical event using the headings in the bio-model.

**Example:**

> **Topic:** Bombardment of Fort Sumter
>
> **Symbol of:** Union Authority
>
> **Four Location Words:** island, harbor, entrance, Charleston
>
> **Five Action Words:** threatened, bombarded, exploded, evacuated, marched
>
> **Caused by:** Confederate demand for a fort in a seceded state
>
> **Valued by:** Both the North and South
>
> **Choices made:** Lincoln's decision to send supplies; Confederate decision to bombard the fort before supplies arrived
>
> **Lacking:** Enough food and supplies to withstand the bombardment
>
> **Major Players:** Union Major Robert Anderson, Confederate authorities
>
> **Simile:** Rubble left was like an abandoned, collapsed mine
>
> **Outcome:** Victory for the South, evacuation of the fort; aroused and united the North

Sentence Sequencing or Cartoon (pp. 117, 122): Show a series of events as cartoons or rearrange sentences to place events in the order in which they happened.

Preposition Report (p. 119). Describe an event using this pattern:

From _____

Through _____

Across _____

Around _____

Between _____

Beneath _____

Near _____

Into _____

# REPORTING ON ANIMALS

Share one or more of the wild and wacky animal tales. Research any animal, and include a description, its food, its habitat, and its habits. Use the information in "A Holiday Story" (p. 142) or "An Infinitive Poem" (p. 137).

**Example:**

### The Grizzly Bear

All I wanted was
to roam freely from Mexico to Alaska
to grow unhindered to my full eight feet and 900 pounds
to find ample game, fish, and berries to satisfy my hunger

to see my silver-tipped brown fur sparkle in the sunlight
to find a cozy den in which to curl up in the winter
to be protected in national parks

But I didn't want
to face big game hunters who kill for sport
to have my head stuffed and placed on a wall
to find my food supply gone as cities spread out
to be confined to s single area, a tiny part of the land I once roamed
to have my beautiful fur made into a rug
to become one of many endangered species

Active research does not always require the use of printed materials. Polls can be excellent avenues for research. To conduct a poll:

1. Determine the data to be gathered. **Example:** Favorite ice cream flavor of students.

2. Determine the population to be polled: Members of one class? Boys only? Girls only? How many?

3. Prepare a chart on which responses are noted.

4. Poll the students. Record responses.

5. Examine responses and draw conclusions.

## QUIZZES

*Wild and Wacky Research* contains several quizzes that can be used to teach the value of determining key words before searching for information. For example (from the "First for Women" quiz on page 68):

Lt. Col. Eileen Collins is the first woman astronaut to _____

Key words: Collins, astronaut

From the Civil War quiz page 103:

The war began when the Southern troops fired on Fort Sumter.

Key words: Fort Sumter

## RESEARCH SKILLS

Although *Wild and Wacky Research* is intended to help students apply those research skills that have been taught, students will enjoy creating wild and wacky excuses using the dictionary and showing their knowledge of the Dewey Decimal System by taking part in library scavenger hunts to complete a wild and wacky story.

# MORE RESEARCH REPORTING MODELS

A quick survey of library/media collections will reveal the titles that follow plus many more product models that will serve as patterns for changing students' research products. In combining the research process with the opportunity to produce something students cannot help but gain both knowledge of the skills and the information needed and of themselves as creative individuals.

*Blunder or Brainstorm: Fact and Fiction of Inventions and Inventors,* by Nancy Polette (Pieces of Learning, 2006).

*Damsel or Daredevil: Fact and Fiction of Famous Women,* by Nancy Polette (Pieces of Learning, 2006).

*The Fighter Wore a Skirt,* by Nancy Polette (Pieces of Learning, 2002).

Narrative poems of 32 American women who faced a challenge and won.

*Fortunately/Unfortunately,* by Remy Charlip (HarperCollins, 1967).

List in chronological order the positive and hegative events in a person's life.

*Gifted or Goof-Off: Fact and Fiction of the Famous,* by Nancy Polette (Pieces of Learning, 2004).

*Iron Horses* or *Covered Wagons, Bumpy Trails,* by Verla Kay (Putnam, 2004).

Both books relate historical events in chronological order, using "Paul Revere" poetry.

*A New England Scrapbook,* by Loretta Krupinski (Harper, 1995).

Shows those things unique to New England, with factual information, poetry, and art.

*Power or Politics: Fact and Fiction of the Presidents,* by Nancy Polette (Pieces of Learning, 2006).

*So You Want to Be President,* by Judith St. George (Philomel, 2000).

Compares names, birthplaces, appearance, personalities, pets, musical ability, athletics, education, and previous jobs of presidents.

*Summer,* by Steven Schnur (Houghton Mifflin, 2000).

An acrostic model for reporting on any topic.

*What Is This Thing?* by Nancy Polette (Pieces of Learning, 2007).

Shows an artifact from 1800s Americana and gives the reader three guesses.

*A World of Wonders,* by J. Patrick Lewis (Dial, 2002).

Clever poems describing well-known places in the world.

# EVALUATION OF RESEARCH PRODUCTS

## Criteria-Based Evaluation

Students are given the criteria for projects or writing assignments on which a grade will be given. The top score for each item is 10 points. There are 10 items, allowing for a perfect score of 100 points. When the student completes the project, he or she scores himself or herself on the criteria. The teacher then scores the project using the same criteria. Student–teacher conferences occur on any criterion about which student and teacher scores differ widely.

## Evaluation of Written Research Products

| | |
|---|---|
| Uses a variety of sources | 1. . . . . . . . . . . . . . . . . . . . . . . . . . . . . . . . 10 |
| Contains factual information backed up by list of sources | 1. . . . . . . . . . . . . . . . . . . . . . . . . . . . . . . . 10 |
| Information is clear | 1. . . . . . . . . . . . . . . . . . . . . . . . . . . . . . . . 10 |
| Is neat and attractive | 1. . . . . . . . . . . . . . . . . . . . . . . . . . . . . . . . 10 |
| Uses correct spelling | 1. . . . . . . . . . . . . . . . . . . . . . . . . . . . . . . . 10 |
| Uses correct punctuation | 1. . . . . . . . . . . . . . . . . . . . . . . . . . . . . . . . 10 |
| Includes details or elaborations | 1. . . . . . . . . . . . . . . . . . . . . . . . . . . . . . . . 10 |
| Uses interesting vocabulary | 1. . . . . . . . . . . . . . . . . . . . . . . . . . . . . . . . 10 |
| Uses correct grammar | 1. . . . . . . . . . . . . . . . . . . . . . . . . . . . . . . . 10 |
| Followed directions | 1. . . . . . . . . . . . . . . . . . . . . . . . . . . . . . . . 10 |

## Evaluation of Nonwritten Products

(Score 1 = no to 10 = yes)

| | |
|---|---|
| Uses a variety of sources | _____ |
| Presents core material in a creative way | _____ |
| Pays attention to detail | _____ |
| Uses a good design (composition) | _____ |
| Draws the eye/how | _____ |
| Logically connects topic and product | _____ |
| Labels and lettering neat and correctly spelled | _____ |
| Is easy to understand | _____ |
| Is accompanied by a list of sources of information | _____ |
| Uses language correctly | _____ |
| Is neat | _____ |

Research activities are keyed to one or more of these national standards:

---

**National Standards in Reading, Language Arts, and Information Literacy**

I. **Reading-Comprehension**
   A. Use prior knowledge to comprehend.
   B. Read to find out, interpret, solve problems.
   C. Understand cause and effect/draw inferences.
   D. Determine main idea and supporting evidence.
   E. Paraphrase/summarize, compare/contrast.
   F. Distinguish fact from opinion.
   G. Use outlines, time lines, graphic organizers.
   H. Connect, react, speculate, interpret, question.
   I. Compare, contrast to support responses.

II. **Writing**
   A. Write to express, discover, reflect.
   B. Write to solve problems.
   C. Choose appropriate form for purpose.
   D. Organize ideas, use precise wording.
   E. Take notes and organize written material.
   F. Recognize and use a variety of nonfiction formats in writing to inform.
   G. Paraphrase and summarize text.
   H. Produce a clearly written, well-developed research report without copying.
   I. Generate and organize ideas.
   J. Develop drafts.
   K. Revise: add, delete, combine, rearrange, edit, proofread, evaluate.
   L. Self-evaluate written products based on specific criteria.

III. **Information Literacy**
   A. Develop questions in response to information needs.
   B. Know characteristics and uses of a wide variety of information sources.
   C. Develop a plan for selecting, evaluating, and using information sources.
   D. Locate and record information. Determine the best method for note taking.
   E. Seek accurate and complete information to make good decisions.
   F. Rearrange findings to create new knowledge and understanding.
   G. Interpret and synthesize information.
   H. Share information and ideas.
   I. Expand knowledge by pursuing information in a variety of forms.
   J. Reflect on strategies; revise and refine.
   K. Develop products and create original works.
   L. Seek information from a variety of perspectives.
   M. Work effectively in groups to develop questions, pursue information, solve problems, and generate knowledge.
   N. Seek out and enjoy a variety of literary experiences.

# Part One

# Food for Thought

## Wacky Food Facts

Americans consume an average of 20 billion hot dogs a year.

A piece of French toast left on his plate by Justin Timberlake was sold on eBay for $3,000.

Chef Boyardee is a real person.

Roasted spiders have three times the protein of cooked beef.

In Mexico the giant water bug is considered a treat.

Favorite pizza toppings in India are pickled ginger, minced mutton, and cottage cheese.

Native Americans boiled and ate the 17-year locust.

A favorite meal in China is bean worms, scorpions, and locusts.

If you visit an African country, you could be served grasshopper egg soup and white ants or weaver moths, eaten with their nest.

Michel Lotito made it into the *Guinness Book of World Records* by eating an entire airplane.

# WACKY VEGETABLES

## AN ONION A DAY KEEPS THE DOCTOR AWAY!

Would you like a high-energy food, low in calories, that helps you avoid *60* diseases? How about a low cholesterol, no fat food that fights the free radicals in your body, which cause destruction to cells? Try the lowly onion!

Are you a B vitamin freak? Want 20 percent of your required vitamin C every day in a food that's low in carbohydrates? Need a potassium fix? Try the lowly onion!

Want to avoid a heart attack? Half of a raw onion a day will raise the good HDL cholesterol 30 percent, increase circulation, lower blood pressure, and prevent blood clotting.

Sounds good, you say, but what about onion breath? Easy! Just chew a little parsley.

## POTATO CHIPS THE RESULT OF AN ANGRY COOK

In 1853 George Crum was a cook at Moon Lake Lodge in Saratoga Springs, New York. One thing that got George's temper up was a customer who sent food back to the kitchen with a complaint. Legend says that Cornelius Vanderbilt, one of the wealthiest men in the nation, dined one night at the Moon Lake Lodge. He ordered fried potatoes and sent them back to the kitchen, saying that they were too thick. The cook sliced some potatoes thinner and sent them out. Once again the plate was returned to the kitchen. The potatoes were still too thick!

George Crum lost his temper. He sliced potatoes in paper thin slices. He fried them so crispy that they could not be picked up with a fork. He grabbed the salt shaker and gave them a good dose of salt. Back the potatoes went to the picky customer. George waited for the explosion. He knew he would probably lose his job. But no explosion came. The potato chips were delicious! Everyone at Vanderbilt's table wanted to try them. It wasn't long before George became famous for his "potato chips."

# RESEARCH REPORT: ODE TO AN ONION

I am an onion
I am clothed in gossamer layers of white
My greatest need is to to guard my chemicals which fight free radicals
My vitamin C cousins are numerous and plentiful
My job is to raise the good type HDL cholesterol
Protein, carbohydrates, sodium, and potassium lurk within my layers
I vacation beneath winter snows
My greatest desire is to increase circulation, lower blood pressure, and prevent blood clotting.
I am an onion!

**Research Project: Standards** I-A; II-D, G; III-D, E F

Choose the potato or another fruit or vegetable. Research its properties, including its nutritional value. Follow this pattern to include as much information as possible.

I am _____

I am clothed in _____

My greatest need is _____

_____

My cousins are _____

My job is to _____

Within my layers are _____

_____

I vacation _____

My greatest desire is _____

_____

I am _____

_____

Source _____

# NEWS RELEASE

This news release appeared in the *St. Louis Post Dispatch* and other major newspapers all over the country on April 1, 1996. How do you know it is a hoax?

<hr>

## Taco Bell Buys the Liberty Bell

In an effort to help the national debt, Taco Bell is pleased to announce that we have agreed to purchase the Liberty Bell, one of our country's most historic treasures. It will now be called the "Taco Liberty Bell" and will still be accessible to the American public for viewing. While some may find this controversial, we hope our move will prompt other corporations to take similar action to do their part to reduce the country's debt.

<hr>

## FAST FOOD FACTS

The first fast-food restaurant opened in the United States on July 7, 1912. It was the New York City Automat. A coin was dropped in a slot and a window opened to reveal the food.

White Castle was the second. It opened in Wichita, Kansas, in 1921. For the first time customers could see the food being prepared. Five holes were added to each beef patty to speed cooking. Hamburgers sold for five cents.

McDonald's was opened by two brothers in 1940 as a barbecue drive in. By 1948 it was famous for its hamburgers, which cost 15 cents. The sandwiches were sold in paper wrapping that could be thrown away.

Wendy's was opened in 1969 in Columbus, Ohio, by Dave Thomas, who learned the fast-food business from Col. Harlan Sanders of Kentucky Fried Chicken fame. Wendy's was the first to have a drive-through window.

# RESEARCH REPORT: FACT OR MYTH?

Here are popular beliefs about food. Research and discover **why** each statement is a fact or a myth. Create a 16-page book titled FACTS AND MYTHS ABOUT FOOD. On one page write a statement about food. Ask whether the statement is a fact or a myth. On the next page give the answer and the evidence (research) that supports the answer. **Standards** I-F; II-C, H; III-D–J

1. Calories eaten at night are more fattening. _____

2. Skipping breakfast helps you lose weight. _____

3. Your body can't tell the difference between honey and sugar. _____

4. Low fat always means low calorie. _____

5. You can eat shellfish on a cholesterol-lowering diet. _____

6. Olive oil has fewer calories than other fats. _____

7. Frozen vegetables are as nutritious as fresh ones. _____

8. Foods boasting "0 trans fat" contain "good" fats. _____

Source: *St. Louis Post Dispatch,* March 21, 2007

## SAMPLE PAGES

| **FACT OR MYTH** | **MYTH** |
|---|---|
| Multigrain foods are always made with whole grains. | "Multigrain" means the product was made with several grains. You can't assume that whole grains were used. |
|  |  |

**Answer Key:** 1, 2, 4, 6, and 8 are myths; 3, 5, and 7 are facts.

# RESEARCH REPORT: KETCHUP ICE CREAM

A Baskin Robbins researcher was watching the popular TV show *All in the Family* and noticed that Archie Bunker, the head of the family, put ketchup on everything, including his breakfast eggs. The researcher decided that because Archie had made ketchup so popular, ketchup ice cream might be a best seller. Baskin Robbins officials thought it was a great idea and created ketchup ice cream. They advertised it as the only vegetable ice cream ever made. They waited for big sales, which never happened. The public preferred their vegetables on their dinner plates and not in the dessert bowl.

Ice cream was invented in the United States in Philadelphia in 1874. George Washington, Thomas Jefferson, and Dolley Madison served ice cream at state dinners. The ice cream cone was invented in 1904 at the World's Fair in St. Louis, Missouri. In 1984 Ronald Reagan declared the month of July to be National Ice Cream Month.

**Take a poll:** your favorite ice cream. Poll ten classmates. **Standards** I-G, H; III-D, G, H

| Name | Chocolate | Vanilla | Strawberry | Other (List) |
|---|---|---|---|---|
| | | | | |
| | | | | |
| | | | | |
| | | | | |
| | | | | |
| | | | | |
| | | | | |
| | | | | |

**Conclusion:** The favorite ice cream flavor revealed in this poll is: _____

Try the same poll with boys, girls, adults, and students in different grade levels. Compare results.

# DICTIONARY SKILLS: THE TV WAS HIS DINNER

Michel Lotito's parents were worried. Their nine-year-old son had strange eating habits. No ice cream and cake for him! He preferred pieces of metal, glass, and even parts of the family TV set. Even today as an adult, an X-ray of Michel's stomach might show parts of bicycles, supermarket carts, or airplanes.

According to CNN news, Michel eats almost anything. He gained a place in the *Guinness Book of World Records* for consuming an entire airplane, a Cessna 150. The champion eater makes his living giving demonstrations of his unusual eating ability. In addition to the airplane, he has eaten 18 bicycles, 18 television sets, and an entire coffin.

Examinations by many doctors reveal that Michel's stomach lining is twice as thick as a normal stomach and that he has suffered no ill effects from his strange diet. Michel says that when not performing, he eats regular meals and is a very good cook.

**Dictionary Fun:** Choose the correct word. **Standards** I-A, B, I

1. The word that best describes Michel's appetite for metal is:

   A) forlorn          B) voracious          C) contagious          D) benign

2. The word that best describes Michel's performance is:

   A) mystical          B) magnificent          C) malevolent          D) astonishing

3. The word that best describes eating an airplane is:

   A) overwhelming     B) ambitious          C) dumb          D) immense

4. The word that best describes Michel's meals at home is:

   A) mundane          B) unusual          C) outrageous          D) original

5. The word that best describes what a doctor looking at Michel's X-ray thinks is:

   A) vast          B) forlorn          C) awesome          D) frightening

6. The word that best describes what Michel's audiences feel is:

   A) revulsion          B) admiration          C) kinship          D) curiosity

7. The word that best describes what Michel does for a living is:

   A) doleful          B) responsible          C) mandatory          D) daring

8. The word that best describes Michel's parents when he was nine is:

   A) unhappy          B) confused          C) courageous          D) taciturn

✂— **Answer Key:** 1-B; 2-D; 3-A; 4-A; 5-C; 6-D; 7-D; 8-B

# RESEARCH REPORT: CHAMPION HOT DOG EATER

Every Fourth of July an International Hot Dog Eating Contest is held at Coney Island in Brooklyn, New York. The women's record for eating 37 hot dogs in 12 minutes is held by Sonya Thomas. Sonya is five foot, five inches tall and weighs 100 pounds, far less than most of her oversized competitors.

Sonya, who manages a Burger Chef restaurant in Maryland, trains for the many competitions she enters. She works out daily on a treadmill and does exercises to improve her hand-eye coordination, jaw strength, and stomach capacity. Twice a week she eats dried squid, a challenge for anyone's jaw. She eats only one meal a day, a chicken sandwich, large fries, and two 42-ounce diet cokes, to keep her stomach stretched. The contests she has won include eating oysters, meatballs, tater tots, and cheesecake. She won the oyster contest by eating 46 dozen oysters in 10 minutes.

**Research the Food Pyramid.** Find out what a healthy diet is. Complete the pattern below. **Standards** II-E, G, I; III-C, D, E, G, H

Sonya's diet (circle one)                 is                 is not                 healthy.

Because _____
_____

Because _____
_____

Because _____
_____

Because _____
_____

Because _____
_____

Because _____
_____

That's why Sonya's diet (circle one)             is             is not             healthy.

# THE GREATEST RECIPE

In 1962 a six-foot, two-inch-tall woman ducked as she walked through the doors of radio station WGBH in Boston. Her name was Julia Child. For the next 30 minutes she talked about her new book, *Mastering the Art of French Cooking.* She mixed in funny stories while she told listeners how to baste, broil, dice, fold, melt, mince, sauté, and simmer all kinds of foods. She made French cooking sound easy. Listeners were so delighted with the recipes she shared that Julia wrote more cookbooks and became the most famous chef of French cuisine in the world, but strangely enough, Julia created her greatest recipe **before** she learned to cook.

When Pearl Harbor was bombed on December 7, 1941, the United States went to war. Julia was determined to go to war, too. She applied to the Navy to join the WAVES. The Navy said NO! She was too tall. Julia landed a job with a new spy agency, the Office of Secret Services (OSS).

In her early days at the OSS Julia worked in the Emergency Rescue Equipment Branch to help pilots and air crews whose planes crashed at sea. Sharks were the greatest danger the downed fliers faced. Sharks smelled the blood of injured flyers and attacked them. Sharks also attacked OSS divers who attached bombs to German U-boats off the Atlantic Coast. Along with others, Julia worked night and day to develop a shark repellent. It needed to be something a flier or a diver could release in the water to drive away the deadly sharks.

Julia did not have to know how to cook to stir up a shark recipe. All she had to do was mix black dye and copper acetate. It smelled like a rotting shark. One whiff of the awful stuff, and attacking sharks turned and swam away. The downed fliers said it was a fine recipe! The OSS divers said it was a marvelous recipe! It was a recipe that saved hundreds of lives. It was Julia's greatest recipe!

# CREATIVE WRITING: WRITING A FABLE

## ABOUT SHARKS

Sharks live in all the oceans but are most numerous in warm seas.

Their scaly bodies can be 40 feet long.

When a shark's tooth is lost, another grows in its place.

Sharks follow ships for days at a time to pick up food thrown overboard.

Some greedy sharks are continuously hunger. As soon as they finish one meal, they look for another.

The 50-foot-long whale shark is harmless to bathers and sailors.

Basking sharks of the Arctic Ocean like to come to the surface and bask in the sun.

White sharks and blue sharks are man eaters.

## ABOUT FABLES

A fable is a short tale, usually featuring two animals. Its purpose is to teach a moral or lesson. **Use the information above** to write a fable featuring sharks. **Standards** I-F; II-C, H; III-D–J

Gliding over the waves of the _____ Ocean was a

_____ shark named _____. Early one morning

_____ was _____ when he spied a

_____ and thought to himself, " _____."

The _____ called out to the _____, saying

"_____."

The _____ replied,

"_____." It was at that moment that

_____. And _____

learned that _____

_____.

# RESEARCH REPORT:
# K RATIONS

**Write a newspaper article** about K rations, another food that came out of World War II. Begin with an interest-catching headline. **Standards** I-E; II-C, D; III-D, E

**HEADLINE** [                                                                  ]

Paragraph One: Who, What, When Where

[                                                                              ]

Paragraph Two: Details

[                                                                              ]

Paragraph Three: Minor Details

[                                                                              ]

# Resources: Food

*Eating,* by Claire Llewellyn. Smart Apple, 2005.
> Why you need to eat; smelling, tasting, digesting.

*Eating Right,* by Helen Frost. Pebble Books, 2000.
> Food guide pyramid with specific foods as examples.

*Fairy Tale Feasts,* by Jane Yolen. Crocodile Books, 2006.
> A literary cookbook for young readers and eaters.

*Food for All,* by Rufus Bellamy. Smart Apple, 2006.
> Actions taken to feed the world's hungry people.

*From Milk to Ice Cream,* by Stacy Taus-Bolstad. Lerner, 2003.
> Step-by-step process in producing ice cream.

*George Crum and the Saratoga Chip,* by Gaylia Taylor. Lee & Low, 2006.
> Legendary tale of the first potato chip.

*The History of Food,* by Judith Jango-Cohen. Twenty-First Century Books, 2006.
> Discusses many methods of preserving foods.

*It's Disgusting and We Ate It!,* by James Solheim. Simon & Schuster, 1998.
> True food facts from around the world.

*Julia Child,* by Laura Shapiro. Viking, 2007.
> Adult biography of the famous chef.

*Junk Food,* by Vicki Cobb. Millbrook, 2005.
> Six snack foods that have little nutritional value.

*Kitchen Science,* by Peter Pentland. Chelsea House, 2003.
> Combines science and food preparation.

*Life and Times of the Peanut,* by Charles Micucci. Houghton-Mifflin, 1997.
> Growing and using peanuts throughout the world.

*The Math Chef,* by Joan D'Amico. Wiley, 1997.
> Sixty math activities and recipes for kids.

*Onions.* by Maria Rogers. Addison-Wesley, 1995.
> A celebration of the onion through recipes, lore, and history.

*Popcorn.* by Elaine Landau. Charlesbridge, 2003.
> Where it came from; nutrition and recipes.

*The Science Chef,* by Joan D'Amico. Wiley, 1995.
> One hundred fun food experiments and recipes for kids.

*The Secret Life of Food,* by Clare Crespo. Hyperion, 2002.
> Preparing food shaped like a variety of objects.

*Where Does Food Come From?,* by Shelley Rotner. Millbrook Press, 2006.
> From field to supermarket, the origin of many foods.

# Part Two

# On the Move!

## Wacky Transportation Facts

The first automobile could not go as fast as a horse and buggy.

The world's largest limousine is 47 feet long and has a built-in swimming pool.

Police in Jackson, Mississippi, pulled over a weaving car driven by a blind driver guided by a drunk passenger.

Fifteen million Model T automobiles were made between 1908 and 1927. All were black.

A bicycle has over 1,000 parts.

It costs a large ship almost $50,000 to go through the Panama Canal.

If the captain applies the brakes to a large ship, it takes three miles to stop.

The first airmail flight in 1918 went by train.

The average American will walk 75,000 miles in a lifetime.

# FLYING

## THE FIRST AIRMAIL FLIGHT: PLANE OR TRAIN?

May 15, 1918, was a day that would go down in history. The first airmail flight from Washington, D.C., to New York was ready to go. President Woodrow Wilson and other important officials gathered for a ceremony to watch the flight take off. Lt. George Boyle, the pilot, was just out of flight school. He was chosen because of family and political connections. After a short speech, President Wilson signed a letter with the first airmail stamp. When the letter arrived in New York it was to be auctioned off for charity.

The pilot turned the switch to start the engine. Nothing happened. He tried a second and third time. Nothing happened. Someone had forgotten to put fuel in the plane! Forty-five minutes later Lt. Boyle took off to the sound of a laughing crowd. Away the plane flew . . . in the wrong direction! After a flight of only 24 miles the pilot was forced to land the plane in a farmer's field, where it flipped over. The young man was not hurt, and the mail was put on a train to its final destination.

## A WALK ON THE WILD SIDE

Rosalie Gordon was a showgirl in Houston, Texas, when the Gates Air Circus came to town. She had done some wing walking earlier with the circus and contacted Ivan Gates about doing the first parachute jump by a woman. Rosalie was hired and preparations were made. The crowd was large as Rosalie climbed out onto the wing and jumped at a signal from the pilot. The girl fell 20 feet and was stopped by a violent jerk. Her parachute had failed to open. She was hung up on a rope still attached to the plane, dangling 20 feet into space. The pilot knew that landing the plane would kill Rosalie, but the fuel supply was low. What could be done? This and many other exciting tales of the early age of aviation are told in *Barnstormers and Daredevils,* by K. C. Tessendorf (Atheneum, 1988).

# RESEARCH REPORT:
# THE AVIATION FIRST NOBODY WANTED

In the First World War, combat planes carried one or two men. On January 6, 1918, Captain Makepeace was on a mission flying over German territory. The other man in the small plane was Captain J. H. Hedley. The trip, flying at 15,000 feet, had thus far been uneventful. Then it happened! Makepeace spotted German aircraft heading straight toward him. He put his plane in a steep dive to avoid the attacking planes. The force of the dive lifted Captain Hedley out of his seat and into the sky. Makepeace assumed that Hedley had fallen to his death as the plane continued to dive several hundred feet before leveling off. It was then that Makepeace heard a thump and felt a drag on the plane's tail. Hedley had fallen in the right spot at the right time. He held on to the tail and soon was able to climb back into his seat, unhurt. Both men were relieved and amazed as Makepeace headed the plane safely back to base.

## Whose Flight Bag Is It?

Here are three flying aces of World War I. Read about each in the encyclopedia. **Match each** with the list of contents of his flight bag. **Standards** I-B, D, H, I

Eddie Rickenbacker          _____

William (Billy) Bishop      _____

Albert Ball                 _____

| 1. | 2. | 3. |
|---|---|---|
| diploma from Trent College | automobile key chain | degree from Royal |
| pilot's certificate | 94th Pursuit Squadron flag | Military College |
| cup with Royal Flying Corps insignia | $10 bill | flag of the 60th |
| flag of the 11th Fighter Squadron | Medal of Honor | Fighter Squadron |
| Victoria Cross | racing trophy | Canadian coin |
| tea bag | Diagram of an internal | Victoria Cross |
| | combustion engine | cane with 72 notches |
| | | lieutenant colonel's hat |
| | | blueberry muffin |

# HIGHLIGHTS IN AVIATION

1903 **Wilbur and Orville Wright** make the first manned powered flight of 852 feet, lasting 59 seconds.

1911 First cross-channel flight, by **Louis Bleriot,** time 37 minutes.

1911 **Harriet Quimby** becomes the first U.S. licensed female pilot.

1921 **Bessie Coleman** becomes the first black female pilot

1926 First U.S. polar flight, with **Richard E. Byrd** as navigator and **Floyd Bennett** as pilot.

1927 **Charles E. Lindbergh** makes the first transatlantic flight in a monoplane.

1932 **Amelia Earhart** makes the first woman's transoceanic solo flight.

1933 First round-the-world solo flight, by **Wiley Post** takes seven days and eighteen hours.

1947 **Charles E. (Chuck) Yaeger** breaks the sound barrier at mach I.

1949 **Capt. James Gallagher** and crew make the first nonstop, around-the-world flight, in *The Lucky Lady II.* They refuel in the air four times.

1973 First female pilot of a major U.S. scheduled airline, **Emily Warner**, is hired by Frontier Airlines as second officer on a Boeing 737.

1998 First female combat pilot to bomb an enemy target, **Lt. Kendra Williams**, USN, bombs enemy targets over Iraq on December 16, during operation Desert Fox.

# RESEARCH REPORT: THE SIMILE REPORT

A simile compares two things using the words like or as. **Example:** Her ambition was as large as an elephant's dream.

**Identify the similes** in the report that follows.

### A Simile Report: Bessie Coleman, 1896–1926

Her family was as poor as an empty piggy bank when her father abandoned her mother and 12 children.

As a child she gobbled up books like a hungry bear awakening in the spring. Her mother taught her to read, knowing that the way out of poverty was education.

Her dream to be a pilot was as impossible as an alligator with feathers, since no black person, and certainly no woman, could qualify as a pilot in 1919.

She felt like a lost piece of luggage when she was turned down by every U.S. flight school because she was black and a woman.

A friend was as generous as a Christmas Santa Claus when he gave her enough money to enroll in a flying school in France.

Her eyes lit up like stars when she earned her pilot's license in 1921 in France, returned to the United States, and was written about in the newspapers.

Her flights were as dangerous as a bull charging a red flag when she performed all over the country as a barnstormer, parachutist, and stunt flyer.

The crowds packed her air shows like a subway car at rush hour to see her daring loops and whirls.

The nation's tears flowed like a river at flood stage when, in 1926, Bessie was thrown out of her plane on a test flight without the parachute she usually wore.

# RESEARCH REPORT: FIRSTS IN AVIATION

## The Simile Report

Select one of these flyers who made aviation history: Orville Wright, Wilbur Wright, Amelia Earhart, Charles E. Lindbergh, Wiley Post, Richard E. Byrd, Harriet Quimby, Emily Warner, Charles (Chuck) Yeager, or Capt. James Gallagher.

Complete a simile report about the person. Follow each simile with information that supports the simile. **Standards** I-A–D; II-A, C, E, G, K; III-D–H

**Create similes** using words from this list or other words of your choice:

| | | | | |
|---|---|---|---|---|
| large | small | rich | poor | happy |
| sad | smooth | rough | strong | quick |
| stubborn | assured | bold | careful | capable |
| clever | confident | curious | determined | eager |
| fearless | innocent | lucky | powerful | relaxed |
| skillful | tough | | | |

Name _____.

His/her family was as _____ as _____.

As a child he/she _____ like a _____.

His/her dreams were as _____ as _____.

One problem was as _____ as _____.

He/she approached _____ like _____

He/she was as _____ as _____ when

_____.

His/her flight(s) was/were as _____ as _____.

The reception of the country was as _____ as

_____ when _____.

Source _____

# RESEARCH SKILLS:
# FIRST TO FLY IN A LAWN CHAIR

To get the complete story, search the library shelves. Find the topic represented by each Dewey Decimal number. **Write the topic in the space next to the number. Standards** III-B

Since the beginning of (1) 529 _____ men have always dreamed of flying. In 1982 a pilot for Pan American (2) 387.7 _____ radioed the Los Angeles tower that he had passed a man in a flying lawn chair with a (3) 355 _____. Radar soon confirmed that it was not a (4) 818 _____. There was an unidentified flying object in the LAX air space flying at 16,000 feet.

The UFO was not from (5) 576.8 _____. It was Larry Walters, who was making his dream of flying come true. Larry bought 45 (6) 551.6 _____ (7) 745.594 _____ and tanks of helium from a local Army-Navy store. He padded his lawn chair and attached the (8) 745.594 _____. Other lines anchored the chair to his (9) 629.2 _____. His plan was to float around a few hours above his house, then pop the (10) 745.594 _____ with his pellet (11) 355 _____ and descend to (12) 550 _____.

Unfortunately, when he cut the lines to take off, he shot up 16,000 feet, and there he drifted for more than 14 hours. Stories vary about how he finally reached (13) 550 _____. One story says that the (14) 745.594 _____ slowly deflated and he came down in Long Beach. Another story says Larry was floating above the (15) 551.46 _____ when a helicopter lowered a rescue line and hauled him to safety. After landing he was arrested for violating LAX air space. Which is true? You will have to ask Larry.

**Answer Key:** 1-time; 2-Airline; 3-weapon (gun); 4-joke; 5-outer space; 6-weather; 7-balloons; 8-balloons; 9-automobile; 10-balloons; 11-weapon (gun); 12-earth; 13-earth; 14-balloons; 15-ocean

# CREATIVE WRITING:
# THE MIRACLE GIRL

**She Went to Bed on One Ship and Awoke on Another!**

The night of July 25, 1956, was the last night of the voyage of the *Andrea Doria*. Sailing from Genoa, Italy, to New York City, the ocean liner carried more than 1,000 passengers. The sea was shrouded in heavy fog. Captain Piero Calamai reduced the ship's speed, activated the warning whistle, and ordered all watertight doors closed.

Sailing east toward Sweden was another ship, the *Stockholm*. Captain Harry Nordenson was not aware of the fog bank that they would soon reach. Without warning, the two ships collided.

Fourteen-year-old Linda Morgan was asleep in her cabin when the *Andrea Doria* was struck broadside. The impact lifted the girl out of her bed, threw her across the two ships, and dropped her, with only a broken arm, on the deck of the *Stockholm* just as the ships scraped past each other and separated. "I was on the *Andrea Doria*," she said. "Where am I now?"

The collision resulted in 51 deaths and hundreds of injuries. Linda's story made headlines throughout the country. She was dubbed "The Miracle Girl."

**Create a cinquain** (five-line poem) about Linda Morgan. **Standards** I-A, B, D; II-A; III-G, H

Line 1: Name _____ Linda Morgan _____

Line 2: Two adjectives _____ _____

Line 3: Three verbs _____ , _____ ,

_____

Line 4: Four-word phrase _____ _____

_____ _____

Line 5: Synonym _____ MIRACLE GIRL! _____

# FAMOUS FIRSTS

## FIRST TO ROW ACROSS THE ATLANTIC OCEAN

How long do you suppose it would take to row an 18-foot boat with no sail from New York to the coast of England? In 1896 George Harbor and Frank Samuelson found out. The trip took 56 days. With plenty of water, canned goods, and extra oars, the two set out on June 6, with each man rowing 18 hours a day. They arrived on the English Coast on August 1. The two were the first, and probably the only, men to achieve such a feat.

## THE FIRST WOMAN TO SAIL ALONE ACROSS THE PACIFIC

On July 26, 1969, hundreds of friends and well-wishers cheered as 39-year-old Sharon Adams sailed her 31-foot ketch into San Diego Harbor. She had left Yokohama, Japan, 74 days earlier and became the first woman to sail alone the 5,618 miles across the Pacific Ocean. When asked how she fought boredom, she answered that she sewed a dress and read 16 books!

## FIRST TO SOUND THE ALARM: RACHEL CARSON, 1907–1964

More than 60 years ago Rachel Carson was concerned about the effects on oceans, rivers, and lakes of chemicals used on crops. Farmers liked DDT and other chemicals. Getting rid of crop pests meant bigger yields. In 1945 Rachel Carson sent an article to the *Readers Digest* pointing out that these chemicals were poisoning the earth and its water bodies. The article was rejected. Carson continued to raise the alarm. Seventeen years after sounding her first warning she found a publisher for her book, *Silent Spring*. Critics called the brave scientist a "hysterical woman," but their voices were stilled when the book became a best seller. Public outcry led to the banning of DDT and other dangerous chemicals.

# RESEARCH MODEL: ANOTHER ALARMIST

### Jacques-Ives Cousteau, 1910–1997

If it had not been for two broken arms, the world might never have heard of Jacques Cousteau. As a youth Jacques gave no thought to scientific studies. He wanted a life of action, so he entered the French Naval Academy. Graduating in 1933, he was on his way to reaching his dream. He would explore the heavens as a navy pilot.

Unfortunately, a terrible automobile accident shattered his dream as well as both of his arms. His recovery was slow, but his strength gradually returned with underwater exercises. Jacques discovered that goggle diving was as exciting as flying. A fascinating undersea world existed that he had never dreamed of. The problem was holding one's breath long enough to enjoy this strange new world. Jacques solved the problem by inventing the aqualung (today called the scuba).

It wasn't enough for Jacques to visit this undersea world again and again. He wanted to share these unbelievable sights with others. He invented the diving saucer and underwater cameras and made film after film that brought the mysteries of ocean life into living rooms everywhere. The money he made from the films was used to buy an old British minesweeper. Jacques and his crew fixed the ship up as a research ship and named it the *Calypso*.

In 1960 Jacques took on a new role as warrior and defender. His undersea world was under attack! The European Atomic Energy Community (the EAEC) announced plans to dump a large amount of radioactive waste into the ocean. The waste would be carried to the ocean by train. Jacques gathered his troops, the people of France. He made them aware of the danger of radioactive waste for ocean life. The French people rose up and joined the protest. Women and children sat on the rails that the train carrying the waste would cross. The train returned to its station.

Thanks to Jacques Cousteau and his "troops," the ocean was saved from that attack.

# RESEARCH REPORT: PROTECTOR OF THE OCEAN

## A Singing Report

After researching the life of a famous person, it can be fun to recall an event in that person's life in song. Some good tunes to use are:

"He's Got the Whole World in His Hands"

"Home on the Range"

"I've Been Working on the Railroad"

"My Bonnie Lies Over the Ocean"

"My Darling Clementine"

**Find out about** the work of Sylvia Earle or Rachel Carson. Write a song about one important event in her life. **Standards** II-E, G, I; III-C, D, E, G, H

**Example: Jacques Cousteau**

Tune: *My Darling Clementine*
O'er the ocean, o'er the ocean
Jacques Cousteau the seas to roam.
Seeking answers, photo-graphing
For he called the ocean home.
Then some people had an idea
They would dump atomic waste.
In the waters of the ocean
Dump it quickly and in haste.
"Bad solution, this pollution,"
Cried out Jacques, so loud and clear.
Led the protest, told the people
Save the oceans we hold dear.
So some mothers and their daughters
When they understood the facts
With great courage, took their bodies
Stretched across the railroad tracks.
Good solution, stopped pollution
Someplace else the waste would go.
Got the message, saved the oceans
Thanks to caring Jacques Cousteau.

# RESEARCH REPORT: WANT TO BUY A CAR?

Ever heard of Nicholas Cugnot? Probably not. Back in 1771 he tried to invent the first automobile. The problem was that it could not go faster than a horse. Folks turned up their noses at poor old Nick's invention.

One hundred years later a French inventor built a car that was powered like a train. It had a steam engine and needed someone other than the driver to add wood to the fire to keep the steam up. Folks turned their noses up at this one, too.

Not to be discouraged, two fellows named Daimler and Benz came up with a gasoline-powered automobile, Its top speed was 10 miles per hour, and the noisy engine scared the horses that pulled buggies, the main means of getting around in those days. Along came Henry Ford. In 1896 he found a way to produce gasoline-powered cars for as little as $700. The automobile was up and running!

Michelle Knapp got the best car deal of all in 1992 when she sold a car that cost her $100 for $50,000 dollars. It happened on October 9, when Michelle heard a loud crash outside her window. When she went to investigate, she saw the trunk of her red Malibu caved in. It had been smashed by a visitor from outer space, a meteorite. She sold the car to R. A. Langheinrich, who exhibits the car all over the world and charges admission to see it.

**Research: Standards** III-E, G

Find the cost today of the lowest priced model of these automobile manufacturers. Read about the features of each.

Ford $_____    Honda $_____

General Motors $_____    Toyota $_____

On the handout on page 28, name the car you would be *least* likely to buy, and tell why.

# RESEARCH REPORT:
# TEN REASONS NOT TO BUY A

_____

Check *Consumer Reports* for information on the four cars researched on the previous page. Choose the one that **least** appeals to you. Give 10 reasons **not** to buy that car. **Standards** I-B, D, F; II-A, B, E, G, L; III-B, D, G, H

1. _____

2. _____

3. _____

4. _____

5. _____

6. _____

7. _____

8. _____

9. _____

10. _____

Source _____

# Resources: On the Move!

*Amazing Aircraft,* by Seymour Simon. Sea Star, 2002
   Easy to read history of aircraft.

*Amazing Flights: The Golden Age,* by Ole Hanson. Crabtree. 2003.
   Barnstormers, women aviators, great air race, and more

*Dangerous Crossings,* by Carol Vogel. Watts, 2003.
   Exciting tales of real-life adventures at sea.

*Disasters at Sea,* by Andrew Donkin. DK Publications, 2001.
   History of famous shipwrecks.

*Flight: The Journey of Charles Lindbergh,* by Robert Burleigh.
   How Lindbergh flew nonstop from New York to Paris in 1927.

*The Great Ships,* by Patrick O'Brien. Walker, 2001.
   Stories of 17 of the world's greatest ships.

*Hear the Train Whistle Blow,* by Milton Melzer. Random House, 2004.
   How the railroad changed the world.

*History of Transportation,* by Judith Herbst. Twenty-First Century Books, 2006.
   Covers transportation from the wheel to the airplane.

*Jacques Cousteau,* by Lesley Dutemple. Lerner, 2000.
   The life and work of the famous undersea explorer.

*Jacques Cousteau and the Undersea World,* by Roger King. Chelsea House, 2001.
   Beautiful photographs of Cousteau's undersea world.

*Mail Call,* by Nancy Bolick. Watts, 1994.
   History of the U.S. Postal Service.

*Rachel Carson,* by Amy Ehrlich. Silver Whistle/Harcourt, 2003.
   Biography of the woman who sounded the alarm about pesticides and the environment.

*Railroad Fever,* by Monica Halpern. National Geographic, 2004.
   The building of the transcontinental railroad.

*The Roads We Traveled,* by Douglas Waitley. Messner, 1979.
   An amusing history of the automobile.

*Robert Fulton and the Development of the Steamboat,* by Morris Pierce. Power-Plus Books, 2003.
   The life, times, and inventions of Fulton.

*Ship,* by David Macaulay. Houghton Mifflin, 1993.
   Step-by-step building of a ship in 1504.

*Talkin' About Bessie,* by Nikki Grimes. Orchard, 2002.

    The story of aviator Elizabeth Coleman.

*The Wright Brothers and Other Pioneers of Flight,* by Ole Hanson. Crabtree, 2003.

    The early pioneers of aircraft building and flight.

# Part Three

# The Doctor Is In!

## Wacky Cures

Pioneers used dried Indian turnip mixed with honey for coughs, but unless the Indian turnip had been scraped from the top downward, the cough mixture would not work.

The root of rhubarb worn on a string around your neck will prevent stomach aches.

Tie a big red onion to the bedpost to keep the person in the bed from having colds.

Put an ax, blade up, under the bed to break the patient's fever.

To cure a sore throat, wear a dirty sock around your neck.

If a toothache is on the left side of your face, a string tied around the little toe of your right foot will stop the ache. For the right jaw, tie the string on the other foot.

Cutting your hair under a new moon will cause baldness.

# CURES WHEN THERE WERE NO CURES

If you were unfortunate enough to get sick 200 years ago, the cures were sometimes worse than the illness. One doctor had a sign that read:

> **John Harlow: Doctor for dogs, cats, horses, and cattle. People welcome.**

Dr. Harlow would likely have suggested the following "cures":

Stroke: Inhale the smoke of a burning pine tree.

Malaria: Eat spider webs before breakfast.

Warts: Rub them with meat, then bury the meat.

Mad dog bite: Hold the key of a church door.

Baldness: Sleep on stones.

Failing vision: Bathe in rainwater collected before dawn.

Colic, gallstones, and arthritis: Wear a copper bracelet.

Headache/fever: Drink the juice of a willow tree.

Toothache: Drive a nail into the tooth until it bleeds, then hammer the nail into a tree (this transferred the pain to the tree.)

To prevent a toothache: Wear a dead mole around your neck.

Only one of these remedies was useful. The juice of the willow tree has another name, salicylic acid, which is the main ingredient in aspirin.

**Take an Internet medical trivia quiz. Standards** I-A

www.triv.net/html/Users3/u8903.htm: A 15-question science quiz, based on *Who Wants to Be a Millionaire?* Questions go from easy to hard.

discoveryhealthcme.discovery.com/quiz/quiz.html: Test your knowledge of medical trivia with this 10-question quiz!

# DICTIONARY PRACTICE: WHY I MISSED SCHOOL TODAY

**Write an excuse** explaining why you missed school today. Use at least 10 of these words correctly in your excuse. Check the dictionary for meanings. **Standards** I-E, I; II-B, D, I, K; III-B, H

| | | | |
|---|---|---|---|
| abdomen | aorta | artery | backbone |
| bacteria | biceps | blood | brain |
| calcium | capillaries | cardiac | cartilage |
| eardrum | enzymes | epidermis | esophagus |
| fever | germs | heart | hemoglobin |
| incisors | ligaments | lungs | metabolism |
| molars | nerves | respiration | retina |
| saliva | spinal cord | stomach | virus |

I missed school today because _____

_____

_____

_____

_____

_____

_____

_____

_____

_____

_____

_____

_____

_____

# QUIZ: AN ELECTRICAL CURE

Being struck by lightning is a terrible thing, but not for Edwin E. Robinson. Robinson was bald, partially deaf, and blind when he was struck by lightning. For reasons still unknown, after the lightning strike he regained his hearing and vision, and his hair even started to grow back (*Montgomery Standard,* August 8, 2007).

**Whole Brain Model**

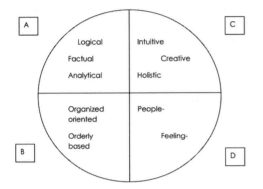

By using electrical probes, researchers have mapped the kind of thinking that occurs in each of the four quadrants of the brain.

Look carefully at the whole brain model. **Indicate which quadrant of the brain is most used** in doing each task listed below by marking A, B, C, or D after each task.

1. Make a plan for completing a task in half the time it usually takes.

2. After reading *Mr. Popper's Penguins,* list facts learned about penguins.

3. What words can you think of that no one else will think of to describe Mary Poppins?

4. Use evidence from the story to predict what will happen next.

5. List events in the story in the order in which they happened.

6. Take part in a jigsaw puzzle contest to see who can complete a puzzle first.

7. Develop a plan to help Miss Muffet get rid of the spider.

8. Give reasons for and against selling candy to raise money for your school.

9. Create an invention that will walk your dog around the block.

10. Describe the feeling you get from listening to Gershwin's "Rhapsody in Blue."

**Answer Key:** 1-B; 2-A; 3-D; 4-A; 5-B; 6-C; 7-B; 8-A; 9-D; 10-C

# DOCTORS

## THE DOCTOR WAS A SPY!

Becoming a woman doctor in the 1850s took a lot of courage. Mary Walker had more than enough! She was one of the first women doctors to graduate from Syracuse Medical College despite the jeers of the male students. But Mary's troubles were only beginning when she opened her office in Rome, New York. The doorbell rarely rang. Her waiting room was empty. No one wanted to be treated by a woman doctor! Along came the Civil War, and Mary went where her skills would be needed. She enlisted in the Union Army, shocked everyone by wearing men's clothing, and went to work as a surgeon in field hospitals. Between patching up head wounds and sawing off legs, she crossed Confederate lines to treat civilians and to bring back vital information. She was taken prisoner in 1864 and spent four months in a Confederate prison. She received the Congressional Medal of Honor from President Andrew Jackson. It was revoked, along with many others, in 1917, but was restored by presidential order in 1977. To this day she is the only woman in U.S. history to receive the Congressional Medal of Honor

## THE DOCTOR WHO WASN'T

In 1964 Frank Abagnale ran away from home at age 16, bought a pilot's uniform, and pretended to be a Pam Am pilot. His pilot's uniform gave him free rides and hotels all over the country for two years. The hoax came to an end when he was asked to fly a plane. Frank disappeared, forged a Harvard Law School diploma, and got a job for one year as an assistant attorney general. That was boring, so for two years he practiced medicine with a forged a medical degree. Not only did he impersonate a doctor, he was so good at it that he became resident supervisor at a Georgia hospital. In five years Frank managed to collect nearly $3 million using forged checks. But the law finally caught up with him. He was jailed, first in France and then in the United States. He regretted his five-year run as a successful con artist and became a model prisoner. However, the authorities thought he was trying to con them and made him serve his full term. Frank now works as a consultant to numerous firms to help them avoid con artists.

# RESEARCH REPORT:
# THE DOCTOR WHO WENT TO JAIL FOR SETTING A BROKEN BONE!

Sounds impossible? It is true that Samuel Mudd was sent to prison for life for setting a bone in the leg of an injured man. Research the life of Samuel L. Mudd. Find the name of the man he helped. Discover the heroic deed that gained his release OR use the same pattern to report on Dr. Mary Walker or Frank Abagnale. **Standards** I-B, D; II-A, D, F; III-B, C, D, E, G

**Use the letters of his name** to tell his story.

S _____

A _____

M _____

U _____

E _____

L _____


L _____


M _____

U _____

D _____

D _____


Source _____

# CREATIVE WRITING: WAS SHE A CRIMINAL?

Mary Mallon was a winsome lass who came to the United States from Ireland in 1883. She got a job as a cook for a wealthy Long Island family. She always had a joke and a smile, and the children adored her. It was not long before 11 people in the house became ill with typhoid fever. Doctors could not find the source of the contaminated food or water that spreads the germ. Mary left the family about three weeks after the outbreak, and no new cases occurred. An investigator hired by the family suspected that Mary was contaminating the food without knowing it. At some time earlier she had had a mild case of typhoid and, while healthy herself, could still spread the disease.

The investigator discovered that in the past 10 years Mary had worked for eight families, and seven had had typhoid outbreaks. The authorities found Mary cooking for a Park Avenue family and imprisoned her in a cottage on the grounds of the Riverside Hospital. After three years she was released but ignored her promise never to cook for others and got a job as a hospital cook. In three months 25 doctors, nurses, and staff members came down with typhoid.

Mary was caught once again and imprisoned in a one-room cottage on Brother Island, where she spent the rest of her life. She worked in the hospital as a cleaning lady and made and sold goods to hospital employees. Among the goods she sold were small cakes she baked!

A diamante is a poem written in the shape of a diamond. It progresses from a short line through lines of increasing length and returns again to a short line.

**Create a diamante** about Mary Mallon. **Standards** I-B; II-G; III-F, G

Name _____

Description: 2 words _____  _____

Action: 3 words _____  _____  _____

Phrase: 4 words _____  _____  _____  _____

Synonym _____

# QUIZ: FIRSTS IN MEDICINE

- First vaccination for smallpox, by Edward Jenner, 1796
- First X-ray machine, Case School of Applied Science, 1896
- First blood transfusion, by Dr. George Crile, 1905
- First heart transplant, by Dr. Christiaan Barnard, 1967
- First face transplant, Isabelle Dinoire, 2005

**Be a medical detective.** Which man in the list below is responsible for each of these famous firsts? Use the almanac to make the matches.

1. Read _____ _____'s portfolio. His vaccine prevented polio.

2. Measles are not around today; thanks to _____ _____ hooray! Hooray!

3. For preventing rabies he had a cure. Let's not forget _____ _____.

4. Antiseptics were his game. _____ _____ was his name.

5. A headache fight he was sure to win; _____ _____ discovered aspirin.

6. For unseen diseases he gave hope, _____ _____ discovered the microscope.

7. For diabetes he was the one; _____ _____ discovered insulin.

8. Penicillin gained him fame; _____ _____ was his name.

A. Alexander Fleming      B. Jonas Salk

C. John Enders      D. Anton van Leeuwenhoek

E. Charles Gerhardt      F. Louis Pasteur

G. Joseph Lister      H. Frederick Banting

**Answer Key:** 1-B; 2-C; 3-F; 4-G; 5-E; 6-D; 7-H; 8-A

# Resources: Medicine

*Catch Me If You Can,* by Frank Abagnale. Mainstream, 2005.

    An impostor takes on the roll of house physician in a major hospital.

*Christiaan Barnard,* by John Bankston. Mitchell Lane Publishers, 2003.

    The story of the first heart transplant.

*A Day in the Life of a Colonial Doctor,* by Laurie Krebs. PowerKids Press, 2004.

    Common ailments of colonial days and how they were treated.

*Death and Disease,* by Alex Woolf. Lucent Books, 2004.

    Description of medicine in the Middle Ages.

*The Disease Fighters,* by Nathan Aaseng. Lerner, 1987.

    The winners of the Nobel Prize in medicine.

*The Doctors,* by Leonard Everett Fisher. Benchmark Books, 1997.

    Medicine in colonial America.

*Edward Jenner, Conqueror of Smallpox,* by Ana Marie Rodriguez. Enslow, 2006.

    Story of Jenner's life and accomplishments.

*Extraordinary Women in Medicine,* by Darlene Stille. Children's Press, 1997.

    Short biographies of women in medicine.

*Frontier Doctors,* by Wyatt Blassingame. Watts, 1963.

    A look at medicine in pioneer days.

*Guinea Pig Scientists,* by Leslie Dendy. Holt, 2005.

    Bold self-experimenters in science and medicine.

*His Name Was Mudd,* by Elden Weckesser. McFarland, 1991.

    The story of Dr. Samuel Mudd.

*Jonas Salk,* by Don McLeese. Rourke, 2006.

    The story of the discoverer of the polio vaccine.

*Joseph Lister,* by Douglas McTavish. Bookwright Press, 1992.

    Story of the father of antiseptics.

*Killing Germs, Saving Lives: The Quest for the First Vaccines,* by Glen Phelan. National Geographic, 2006.

    Includes information on several famous scientists.

*Mary on Horseback,* by Rosemary Wells. Dial, 1998.

A brave woman goes into the depths of the Appalachian Mountains to bring medical care to the people there for the first time.

*Medicine,* by Jen Green. Blackbirch Press, 2004.

A history of medicine from ancient times to the present.

*The President Is Shot! The Assassination of Abraham Lincoln,* by Harold Holzer. Boyds, Mill, 2004.

Details of the end of Lincoln's life, including the unjust arrest of Samuel Mudd.

*The Story of Mary Walker,* by Carla Johnson. Morgan Reynolds, 2007.

The story of the woman doctor who served during the Civil War.

*The Story of Medicine from Acupuncture to X Rays,* by Judy Lindsay. Oxford University Press, 2003.

A history of medicine from ancient times to today.

*Typhoid Mary,* by Anthony Bourdin. Bloomsbury, 2005.

The story of Mary Mallon who, as a hired cook, infected dozens of people with typhoid fever.

*Why Don't Haircuts Hurt?,* by Melvin Berger. Scholastic, 1999.

Questions and answers about the human body.

# Part Four

---

# Crime Doesn't Pay

## Wacky Crime Facts

Eugene Vidocq, a hardened criminal, became head of the French detective branch, the Sureté.

In 1592, John Popham, a robber, became Chief Justice of England.

A trespasser who stopped traffic for hours by sitting in the middle of a San Antonio highway served no jail time.

In Alabama carrying a comb in your pocket can get you arrested, because it may be used as a weapon.

In Michigan, it is against the law to chain an alligator to a fire hydrant.

In Fairbanks, Alaska, a man went to jail for walking his moose on the sidewalk.

# QUIZ: CRIME DOESN'T PAY

- A FELONY is a crime punishable by a prison sentence of more than one year.

- A MISDEMEANOR is a crime punishable by either a fine or a shorter stay in the local jail, or both.

**State** whether each of the following is a FELONY OR MISDEMEANOR. **Standards** I-C, D, F, I

## 1. Following the Rules

In May 2007 Christopher Emorey was sentenced to two years in prison for robbing a Peterborough, Ontario, bank from which he had intended to take $2,000. However, the teller said she could give him only $200 and also must take out a $5 fee because he was not a regular customer. Emorey stood stoically while she did the paperwork and then handed him $195, which he took and walked away (only to be arrested a short time later) (*St. Louis Post Dispatch,* August 7, 2007).

## 2. Bomb Threat

According to the *Savannah (GA) Morning News,* it was no problem to locate and arrest two teenagers who called in a bomb threat at Southwestern Middle School. The teens broke into a house while the homeowner was gone and used the phone in the house to call in the threat. Of course, the 911 system has up-to-date equipment that can trace the location of any phone call received. When police arrived, they found the home had been burglarized and three teens were nearby with the loot. Two were arrested but one got away . . . probably not for long.

## 3. Hospital Visitor

A man was hospitalized for separate wounds in Knoxville, Tennessee, on July 1, 2, and 3, 2007. He was hit by a car one night, then released from the hospital the next day, but was back after an intruder attacked him in his home. After his release the next day he was back again. The police had shot him as he took part in an attempted robbery (*St. Louis Post Dispatch,* August 6, 2007).

## 4. This Is a Hold-Up

A car pulled up and stopped in the deposit lane of a Fairfax County, Virginia, bank. The teller saw a man put a note in the vacuum tube and send it through. Imagine her surprise when she read, "Put all your money in the tube and send it back. This is a hold up." The teller sent the note back without the cash and the criminal drove away. (*St. Louis Post Dispatch,* May 31, 2007).

**Answer Key:** Number 2 is a misdemeanor; 1, 3, and 4 are felonies.

# RESEARCH REPORT: INTRUDER CAUSES TRAFFIC JAM . . . NO TICKET GIVEN

Loop 410 in San Antonio, Texas, is generally a busy highway. Traffic jams are common and motorists are resigned to frequent tie-ups. On May 4, 2007, near the end of the rush hour, a huge traffic jam resulted when a scaly, sharp-toothed creature decided to take a walk down the freeway. Cars came to a screeching halt when confronted by a 7.9-foot alligator sunning itself in the middle of the road. The alligator bit a piece off the bumper of the first police car to arrive on the scene. Police tried scaring the critter off with sirens and by throwing orange traffic cones. The alligator didn't budge. The game warden was called. Finally, using a lasso and long poles, police coaxed the creature into a ditch leading to a lake. No tickets were issued. Motorists late to work may have had a hard time getting the boss to believe their tardiness was due to an alligator.

**Underline** three of these statements that are NOT true. Guess if you do not know. Support or deny your guesses by reading about alligators in the encyclopedia. Correct the untrue statements.

1. Alligator attacks occur in or near fresh or brackish bodies of water.

2. Avoid swimming outside of posted swimming areas or in waters that might be inhabited by large alligators.

3. Alligators are most active during daylight hours.

4. When fed, alligators overcome their natural wariness and learn to associate people with food.

5. Throwing fish scraps in the water is a good way to feed alligators.

6. Dogs are more susceptible to being attacked than humans, because dogs resemble the natural prey of alligators.

7. It is safe to keep a baby alligator as a pet.

**Corrections**

_____

_____

_____

_____

🔑 **Answer Key:** Numbers 3, 5, and 7 are not true.

# MASTER CRIMINALS TURNED DETECTIVES

## ROBBER TO CHIEF JUSTICE

Who would know the ways of criminals better than a criminal? Walking alone down a dark London street in 1585 was a dangerous undertaking. The unlucky walker might well be waylaid by John Popham. John was a law student with reckless and expensive habits. Being an adventuresome young man, he bought a pistol and waited on the dark, foggy London streets for unwary passersby, whom he robbed of their possessions. Ten years later, having obtained his law degree and gained a reputation as an excellent prosecutor, John became the Chief Justice of England, deciding on the fates of hundreds of criminals.

## "*LES MIS*" BASED ON A REAL CRIMINAL

When Victor Hugo wrote *Les Misérables,* his inspiration for the main character was Eugène François Vidocq. As a young man Eugene was a bandit and faced arrest many times. More often than not he escaped, but when he was arrested for smuggling, he was sent to prison for eight years at hard labor. He escaped from the galleys and set out to sea. Another sailor recognized him and turned him in to authorities. Vidocq offered to become a spy for the French police if he could stay out of prison. Using many disguises, he formed a plainclothes unit of former criminals. He worked as a detective for 23 years, eventually becoming head of the French Detective Bureau, the Sûreté. Along with Sir Robert Peel, Vidocq also helped to establish Great Britain's famous Scotland Yard.

## PLAY THE SCOTLAND YARD BOARD GAME ON THE INTERNET

**Standards** I-C, D, F

en.wikipedia.org/wiki/Scotland_Yard_(board_game). "Scotland Yard" is a board game in which a team of players, as "police," cooperate to track down a player controlling a "criminal" around a board.

# RESEARCH REPORT: OUTLAWS OF THE WILD WEST

## BILLY THE KID, 1859–1881

Billy the Kid was born William H. Bonney in New York City. He moved to Silver City, New Mexico, in 1871. He was self-taught. He killed his first man with a pen knife. He worked for both sides in the Lincoln County Cattle Wars. He vowed to avenge the death of his friend, John Tunstall and became a gunslinger and outlaw. He was killed by his friend, Pat Garrett, sheriff of Lincoln County, after escaping from Garrett's jail.

## WYATT EARP, 1848–1929

In the 1870s hew was arrested in Indian Territory for stealing horses. In 1875 he was kicked off the police force in Wichita, Kansas, for keeping the fines he collected. Hw was run out of town in Las Vegas, Nevada, for trying to work a "gold brick swindle." He became deputy sheriff of Tombstone, Arizona, in 1880. and was involved in the OK Corral gunfight. In 1882 he was involved in claim jumping in California. Earp was known as an outlaw, wanderer, and sometime lawman.

**Find more information** about these men of the Wild West and complete the patterns below. **Standards** I-B, C, D, E; II-A, D, E, G; III-C, D, E, G

### The Who, What, When, Where, Why Acrostic

Billy the Kid

| | | |
|---|---|---|
| (who) | B | _____ |
| (what) | I | _____ |
| (when) | L | _____ |
| (where) | L | _____ |
| (why) | Y | _____ |

Wyatt Earp

| | | |
|---|---|---|
| (who) | W | _____ |
| (what) | Y | _____ |
| (when) | A | _____ |
| (where) | T | _____ |
| (why) | T | _____ |

# RESEARCH SKILLS: MYSTERY SCAVENGER HUNT

## THE OUTLAW JESSE JAMES

There are many tales told about Jesse James. Some say he was a modern-day Robin Hood who stole from the rich and gave to the poor. Others say he was a no-good bank robber. Here is one of the legends about him.

**Search the library shelves.** Find the topic represented by each Dewey Decimal number. Write the topic in the space next to the number. **Standards** III-B

Jesse James and his gang were the (1) 303.6 _____ of the Old (2) 978 _____. They hid out in (3) 551.4 _____ and tore through towns like a (4) 551.55 _____, destroying everything in their path.

One day Jesse and his gang rode up to a dilapidated (5) 630.1 _____. They saw one old sway-backed (6) 636.1 _____ and two skinny (7) 636.7 _____ that looked like they hadn't been fed in days.

An old woman came to the door. She had just returned from the (8) 393 _____ of her husband. She told Jesse that she owed the landlord $1,500 on the mortgage. She could not pay and she and her children would be thrown off the (9) 630.1 _____ that very day.

Jesse gave her the (10) 3324 _____. The grateful woman gave Jesse and his men some (11) 363.8 _____ and they rode off into the (12) 582.116 _____

The landlord collected the (13) 332.4 _____ and as soon as he was away from the house, Jesse attacked the man and stole the $1,500 back from him.

**Answer Key:** 1-terrorists; 2. West; 3-caves; 4-hurricanes; 5-farm; 6-horse; 7-dogs; 8-funeral; 9-farm; 10-money; 11-food; 12-trees; 13-money

# GUILTY OR INNOCENT?

## TOKYO ROSE

Soldiers stationed in the Pacific in World War II often listened to Tokyo Rose on a Japanese radio station. In soft tones she urged the soldiers to go home to their sweethearts because many of their ships were sunk and the war in the Pacific Ocean was lost. The American soldiers did not take Tokyo Rose seriously and liked the popular American tunes she played.

Iva Toguri was American born, graduated from Compton Junior College and was sent to Japan Fast Facts: Bornjust before the war by her family to care for a sick aunt. When the war broke out she could not return home. Because she was American, the aunt wanted her arrested as a traitor to Japan. Instead she was forced to work by the Japanese on an English-language radio program. She refused to renounce her U.S. citizenship and risked her life purchasing food and medicine for three American prisoners of war. Her broadcasts were few. Her scripts were written by one of the POWs, who assured her that they contained nothing damaging to the morale of the American soldiers. Nineteen other women of Japanese citizenship broadcast to the soldiers as well. All were given the name Tokyo Rose.

After the war Iva Toguri was arrested and found guilty as the voice of the infamous Tokyo Rose. She was sentenced to 10 years in prison. Guilty or innocent? What do you think?

## AXIS SALLY

American-born Mildred Sisk worked as an English-language instructor in Germany in 1935 when she got a job as an announcer for Radio Berlin. When the war broke out, her broadcasts to American soldiers taunted them about their wives back home and voiced concern about the physical state of captured and wounded soldiers, whom she called by name. She posed as a Red Cross worker and recorded messages of prisoners/soldiers for broadcast. The messages were distorted with added propaganda. An aspiring actress, she played a part in a realistic radio drama about a foiled invasion of France.

In 1949 she was tried for treason and found guilty. She was sentenced to 10 to 30 years in jail. In 1961 she was released on parole. "Axis Sally," as she was called by the soldiers, died at age 87 in 1988. Guilty or innocent? What do you think?

# CONCLUSION PAPER: THE PERSUASIVE ESSAY

**Find more information** about Tokyo Rose or Axis Sally. Complete the outline below for a persuasive essay to convince the jury of the guilt or innocence of one the women. **Standards** I-B, C, F, H, I; II-D, E; III-D, E, F, L

**Facts and Opinions.** Opinions are based on your thoughts or feelings. Facts are gathered from research, reading, or experience.

**Make an Outline**

Name _____

1. Introduction/Thesis Statement _____

_____

2. Supporting Reason 1 _____

_____

Supporting Detail _____

_____

Supporting Detail _____

_____

3. Supporting Reason 2 _____

_____

Supporting Detail _____

_____

Supporting Detail _____

_____

4. Conclusion (strong restatement of thesis or summary of the main points)

_____

_____

# Resources: Crime

*America's Dumbest Criminals,* by Allan Butler. Gramercy Publishers, 2000.
> True accounts of crimes gone wrong.

*Axis Sally: Treacherous Traitor,* by Nathan Aaseng. Oliver Press, 1997.
> The life and times of Mildred Sisk, better known as Axis Sally.

*The Bone Detectives,* by Milton Meltzer. Little Brown, 1996.
> How science is used to solve crimes.

*Case Closed,* by Milton Meltzer. Orchard Books, 2001.
> Methods used by detectives to solve crimes.

*Crime and Detection,* by Brian Lane. Dorling Kindersley, 2005.
> Describes crime-solving strategies.

*The FBI Director,* by Scott Ingram. Blackbirch Press, 2004.
> Describes the job of the head of the Federal Bureau of Investigation.

*Forensic Science,* by Peter Pentland. Chelsea House, 2003.
> Science applied to solving crimes.

*Great Unsolved Cases,* by Arnold Madison. Watts, 1978.
> Unsolved cases from, Jack the Ripper to the disappearance of Flight 967.

*Guilty or Innocent?,* by Anita Gustafson. Holt, 1985.
> The reader guesses the verdict of famous cases.

*In the Line of Fire,* by Judith St. George. Holiday House, 1999.
> Presidents lives in danger, and how the president is protected.

*Major Unsolved Crimes,* by Brain Innes. Mason Crest Publishers, 2003.
> Six challenging cases that have frustrated investigators.

*Pinkerton: America's First Private Eye,* by Richard Wormser. Walker, 1990.
> Biography of Allan Pinkerton.

*Safety in Your Neighborhood,* by Lucia Raatma. Child's World, 2005.
> Ways to keep safe in everyday life.

*The Stupid Crook Book,* by Leland Gregory. McMeel Publishing, 1972.
> Hilarious true tales that show crime doesn't pay.

*Thieves!,* by Andreas Schroeder. Annick Press, 2005.
> Ten stories of surprising heists, comical capers, and daring escapades.

*Tokyo Rose: Orphan of the Pacific,* by Masayo Duns. Kodansha International, 1983.
>Story of a young woman caught between two cultures.

*The Wildlife Detectives,* by Donna Kallner. Houghton Mifflin, 2000.
>How forensic scientists fight crimes against nature.

*The Young Detective's Handbook,* by William Butler. Little, Brown, 1981.
>Fundamentals of crime investigation.

# Part Five

# The White House

## Wacky White House Facts

George Washington had to borrow money to go to his own inauguration.

The six white horses in Washington's stables had their teeth brushed every morning.

The Executive Mansion was torched in August 1814 when the British stormed Washington, D.C. The inside was gutted but the outside was saved by a rainstorm.

Those who rebuilt the structure painted the fire-blackened walls white, creating the new name, White House.

George Washington was the only president who never lived in the White House.

Thomas Jefferson kept bears in cages on the White House lawn.

The children of Teddy Roosevelt used the East Room as a roller skating rink. The sports-minded president held a boxing match there.

It takes a staff of 91 people to run the White House today.

# THOSE SURPRISING PRESIDENTS

Some presidents favored unusual animals for pets.

Thomas Jefferson, a widower, listened all day to his pet mockingbird rather than a wife. He also kept two grizzly bear cubs on the White House lawn.

Martin Van Buren had two tiger cubs.

James Buchanan topped that with a pet elephant.

Calvin Coolidge had a pet pygmy hippo.

John Quincy Adams swam nude each morning in the Potomac River. Hopefully he left his pet alligator at home.

Andrew Johnson could barely read and could not write at all when he became president. His wife, a schoolteacher, taught him to write.

As a boy Ulysses S. Grant hated hunting and despised the sight of blood.

Grover Cleveland kept it a secret from everyone that doctors replaced the bone in his jaw with a bone made of rubber.

Teddy Roosevelt, who wrote a popular book about his fighting in Cuba, only fought one day.

Harry Truman was born with flat eyeballs and had to wear thick glasses all his life.

The largest president was William H. Taft. Over six feet tall, he weighted 325 pounds and got stuck in the White House bathtub the first time he tried to take a bath.

Ronald Reagan, known to like jelly beans, handed them out freely to his staff, saying that they would give them energy to get more work done.

President Roosevelt's dog Fala got so many letters he had to have his own secretary. He had a bone every morning, brought on the president's breakfast tray. He traveled with the president on important trips to Newfoundland, Mexico, and the Aleutian Islands. In April 1945 Fala attended the president's funeral.

# RESEARCH REPORT: FAVORITE SONGS

Which president would choose which Grammy award–winning song as his favorite? Why?
**Standards** I-B, H, I; II-I; III-D, E, G

**Example:** "Two Against Nature": Jimmy Carter. Jimmy and his wife Rosalyn were partners in every way. She rarely left his side and provided input for many of his decisions. They paid no attention to public opinion or a Congress that felt her role in decision making was inappropriate.

1. "I Try" _____

2. "Both Sides Now" _____

3. "There Goes the Neighborhood" _____

4. "With Arms Wide Open" _____

5. "Change the Word" _____

6. "All I Wanna Do" _____

7. "Wind Beneath My Wings" _____

8. "Don't Worry, Be Happy" _____

Any answer that can be justified is acceptable. Sources can be listed on the back of this sheet.

# THOSE SURPRISING FIRST LADIES!

## DID YOU KNOW?

Abigail Adams hung her wash in the East Room, where the president's flapping underdrawers greeted visitors like an official flag.

Dolley Madison loaded wagons with White House treasures, leaving her personal things behind, as she escaped just before the British arrived and burned the White House.

Angelica Van Buren, the president's daughter-in-law, served as his hostess, sitting on a throne. She thought she was a princess!

Abigail Fillmore was her husband's schoolteacher when he was a teenager.

Julia Grant had a roving eye that jumped around. Her husband forbade her to have it fixed, thinking an operation was too dangerous.

Lucy Hayes forbade spirits and tobacco in the White House. She served only lemonade and got the nickname "Lemonade Lucy."

Frances Cleveland's first child was named Ruth, and the Baby Ruth candy bar was named for the child.

Caroline Harrison and her husband refused to touch a light switch, thinking that they might be electrocuted.

Ida McKinley knit 3,000 pairs of slippers during her time in the White House.

Helen Taft refused to have bald waiters serve at the White House dinners.

Mamie Eisenhower loved pink. White House decorations were changed to reflect that color.

Betty Ford danced professionally on Broadway.

Nancy Reagan consulted an astrologer before allowing her husband to make appointments or schedule trips.

# RESEARCH REPORT: THE FIRST LADIES

Choose one of the first ladies and tell about an important part of her life in rhyming poetry, with no more than two or three words per line.

See the example given for Ellen and Edith Wilson. **Standards** III-D, G, H

**Name**
_____

Ellen Wilson
Very thrifty
Edith Wilson
Clothes were nifty
Ellen gracious
Shy and caring
Edith somewhat
Wild and daring
Ellen read books
Every day
Then sad to say
She passed away.

Edith was
The second wife
Perfect for
Political life.
Woodrow grew so
Very ill
Edith did
His job until
He got better
Lucky man
Edith pulled off
Quite a sham.
She held off
A curious mob
That was how
She saved his job.

Ellen Axon Wilson (1860–1914)
First lady 1913–1914
Edith Boling Galt Wilson (1872–1961)
First lady 1915–1921
First and second wives of Woodrow Wilson

# GHOSTS IN THE WHITE HOUSE

The curse of the long-deceased Native American Chief Tecumseh, lingered over the White House for many years. Tecumseh was angry with decisions made by President Benjamin Harrison and placed a curse on him and future presidents. The curse said that any president elected in a year that ended with 0 would die in office. These presidents fulfilled the curse: Abraham Lincoln, 1860; James Garfield, 1880; William McKinley, 1900; Warren G. Harding, 1920; Franklin D. Roosevelt, 1940; John F. Kennedy, 1960.

There is an often repeated tale that Abraham Lincoln had a dream about his death. He went into the East Room, where he saw a casket and heard the mourners. When he asked who was in the casket, an attendant told him that President Lincoln had been killed by an assassin.

Many Lincoln sightings have been reported in the White House. President Coolidge's wife, Grace, says she saw Lincoln standing at the window of the Oval Office. Queen Wilhelmina answered a knock on her bedroom door to see Lincoln standing there. Mrs. Roosevelt's secretary saw Lincoln sitting on a bed pulling on his boots.

The warmest room in the unfinished White House when Abigail Adams became the first lady was the East Room. That was where she hung her wash to dry. Several staff members have reported seeing Abigail hurrying toward the East Room with her wash.

Dolley Madison loved flowers and had rose bushes planted on the White House grounds. The roses can be seen today thanks to her ghost. First lady Edith Wilson told the gardeners that the rose bushes should be dug up. Before a spade was put in the ground, the gardeners reported that the ghost of Dolley Madison appeared to protect her roses. The gardeners dropped their spades and ran away.

Other ghostly sightings include Andrew Jackson, who was said to march through the halls cursing, and David Burns, who gave the government the land on which the White House was built.

These tales and many others can be found on numerous Internet sites. Search using the words White House Ghosts.

# CREATIVE WRITING: CREATE A WHITE HOUSE GHOST STORY

Choose an actual White House family as your characters. Descriptions of the characters should be accurate. **Standards** I-A, D

**Complete this outline.**

**Title** _____

**Characters: Short Description**

1. _____ _____

2. _____ _____

3. _____ _____

4. Who is the ghost? _____

**Setting:** The White House

When? _____

What room or rooms? Description must be accurate. _____

_____

**Plot:** State the story problem. _____

_____

Why is the ghost haunting the White House? _____

_____

What problem does this present for the occupants? _____

_____

List three events that take place before the problem is solved.

1. _____

2. _____

3. _____

How is the problem solved? _____

_____

_____

# QUIZ: THE WHITE HOUSE

Read about the White House in the encyclopedia or check out the *Wikipedia* article on the White House on the Internet. **Place the correct numbers in the blank spaces.** Total all the numbers. If your answers are correct, the total should be 1,570,683. **Standards** I-A; III-D

1. Thomas Jefferson, president number _____, submitted plans for the first Executive Mansion, but his plans were rejected.

2. The architect for the first Executive Mansion was James Hoban, who won a $_____ prize.

3. The Executive Mansion was built on _____ acres of land, donated by a private citizen.

4. John Adams, president number _____, was the first president to occupy the Executive Mansion.

5. The British burned down the Executive Mansion in 1812. Dolley Madison, wife of president number _____, saved many of the furnishings before fleeing.

6. Following his inauguration, _____ people followed Andrew Jackson into the Executive Mansion. They stole or broke thousands of dollar' worth of plates, cups, and silver.

7. Jackson spent $_____ dollars to repair the damage done by the crowds.

8. Theodore Roosevelt, president number _____, was the first to name the Executive Mansion the White House.

9. Today the White House has _____ rooms.

10. _____ people visit the White House annually.


Total of all numbers _____

⚷━★ **Answer Key:** 1-3; 2-$500; 3-18; 4-2; 5-4; 6-20,000; 7-50,000; 8-26; 9-130; 10-1.5 million

# Resources:
# The Presidents and Their Wives

**Standards** III-N

*Bill Clinton,* by Tim O'Shei. My Report Links, 2003.

*Dwight D. Eisenhower, Young Military Leader,* by George Stanley. Simon & Schuster, 2006.

*Eleanor Roosevelt,* by Russell Freedman, Clarion, 1993.

*Franklin Delano Roosevelt,* by Russell Freedman, Clarion, 1990.

*George H. W. Bush,* by Tim O'Shei. My Report Links, 2003.

*George W. Bush,* by Sandra Kachureck. Enslow Publishers, 2004.

*Gerald R. Ford Library and Museum.* Power Kids Press, 2004.

*Great Little Madison,* by Jean Fritz. Putnam, 1989.

*Harry S. Truman,* by George Stanley. Simon & Schuster, 2004.

*Jacqueline Kennedy Onassis: Friend of the Arts,* by Beatrice Gormley. Simon & Schuster, 2003.

*James Monroe,* by Tim O'Shei. My Report Links, 2002.

*Jimmy Carter,* by Deborah Kent. Children's Press, 2005.

*John Adams,* by Cheryl Harness. National Geographic Society, 2003.

*John and Abigail Adams,* by Judith St. George. Holiday House, 2001.

*John F. Kennedy Library and Museum,* by Amy Margaret. Power Kids Press, 2004

*Lincoln: A Photobiography,* by Russell Freedman. Clarion, 1987.

*Old Hickory: Andrew Jackson and the American People,* by Albert Marrin. Dutton, 2004.

*Ronald Reagan Library and Museum,* by Amy Margaret. Power Kids Press, 2004.

*Theodore Roosevelt: Champion of the American Spirit,* by Betsy Harvey. Clarion, 2003.

*Thomas Jefferson,* by Matt Doeden. Graphic Library, 2006.

*Where Washington Walked,* by Raymond Bial. Walker & Co., 2004.

# Part Six

# People Who Were First

## Crazy Firsts

Maria Telleria, a border observer at the Gaza–Egypt border, reports a first: a woman who tried to cross the border with three crocodiles strapped to her waist.

Rescuers in Germany reported a 91-year-old man as the first they had to pry loose from the tar on his roof. He was retarring the roof when he slipped and got stuck.

In 1935 three boys who were shoveling snow were the first to rope an alligator and pull it out of a New York City sewer.

Elizabeth Blackwell was the first woman to be admitted to a U.S. medical school. She was accepted as a result of a joke. She graduated first in her class.

On July 11, 1962, Fred Baldasare became the first man to swim the English Channel UNDERWATER!

# MORE CRAZY FIRSTS

## KATE SHELLEY: THE FIRST GIRL TO STOP A TRAIN WRECK

Would you like to have a bridge named after you? Kate Shelley did. Kate was born on an Iowa farm in 1881. She was a tomboy who rode bareback and shot hawks. She liked to dance across the railroad bridge that spanned the roaring Des Moines River. There was little time for dancing, however, because Kate's days were spent plowing and planting and running the family's small farm. Her father was dead and her mother was an invalid.

One stormy winter night in 1896 part of the railroad bridge collapsed under the weight of the ice that had accumulated. The next train was due in one hour. There was no way the engineer could see that the bridge was out before it was too late. The only way the engineer could be warned was by telegraph. Kate knew what she had to do. Holding a kerosene lamp in one hand, she crawled on hands and knees across the remaining part of the icy bridge to get to town with a warning. A telegraph operator reached the train in time. Brave Kate saved the lives of all the passengers on the train. In gratitude, the state of Iowa named the new bridge after Kate.

## MAY PIERSTORFF: THE FIRST PERSON TO BE MAILED

May Pierstorff was four years old in 1914 in Grangeville, Idaho. Her parents wanted to send her to visit her grandmother in Lewiston but could not afford the train fare. They solved the problem by taking her to the post office and mailing her, which cost 53 cents. The postmaster consulted his rule books but could find no rule about mailing children. The rules did say that baby chicks could be mailed, so he listed May as a baby chick and attached the stamps to May's coat. The little girl traveled in the baggage car with the rest of the mail. When she reached her destination, a postal clerk, Leonard Mochel, delivered her to her grandmother's house.

# QUIZ: AMAZING FIRSTS FOR WOMEN

What "first" can each of these women claim? **Standards** I-A; III-D

1. 1872: Victoria Woodhull becomes the first woman to run for

_____

2. 1925: Nellie Ross becomes the first woman to be elected

_____

3. 1926: Gertrude Ederle is the first woman to swim

_____

4. 1931: Amelia Earhart is the first woman to fly

_____

5. 1960: Oveta Culp Hobby, director of the Women's Army Corps in World War II, is the first woman to receive

_____

6. 1969: Shirley Chisholm of New York is the first African American woman elected to

_____

7. 1970: Diane Crump becomes the first female jockey

_____

8. 1981: Sandra Day O'Connor is the first woman to be appointed to

_____

9. 1999: Lt. Col. Eileen Collins is the first woman astronaut to

_____

10. 2005: Condoleezza Rice becomes the first African American female

_____

**Answer Key:** 1-president of the United States; 2-governor of a state; 3-the English Channel; 4-solo across the Atlantic Ocean; 5-U.S. Army's Distinguished Service Medal; 6-Congress; 7-to ride in the Kentucky Derby; 8-the Supreme Court; 9-command a space shuttle mission; 10-secretary of state

# RESEARCH REPORT: A RAP

Choose one of the women who was first in her field (listed on page 68). Complete this information about her. **Standards** I-B, C, D; II-A, G; III-D, G, H

**A [Name]** _____ **Rap**

One there was a woman. _____ was her name.

She was born in (State) _____. _____

was her game. (area of expertise)

As a child she _____, so it would seem.

She worked and she worked to achieve her dream.

Go, girl go! There's no time for play or having fun.

Go, girl, go! For you'll soon be **NUMBER ONE!**

Now (first name) _____ was smart, yes, she was no fool.

_____ is where she went to school.

The course she set was firm and steady.

Then in (year) _____ she proved she was ready.

She was the first to _____, as you can see.

And that is why (name) _____ went down in history.

Go, girl go! Now there's time for play and having fun.

Go, girl, go! Now they call you NUMBER ONE!

# MORE LITTLE-KNOWN FIRSTS

## THE DAREDEVIL PILOT KNOWN FOR HIS "FIRSTS"

Beachy was a barnstorming pilot who thrilled crowds with his daring stunts. His label everywhere he went was "The Man Who Owns the Sky." He was the first to turn his plane upside-down and fly in that position. He was the first to put his plane into a continuous loop. When he flew over Niagara Falls, he dove under the "Honeymoon Bridge." He thrilled fans by aiming his plane at high speed straight for the ground and then pulling up at the last minute. He called the stunt the "Dip of Death." When he was bet that he couldn't fly under the Golden Gate Bridge, he took the bet. He not only was the first to do so, but "looped-the-loop" under and over the bridge. In one year, 1913 to 1914, he supposedly entertained more than 17 million people.

## THE FIRST MAN TO LIFT 6,000 POUNDS

It was no surprise that Paul Anderson was called "the strongest man in the world." Paul was five feet, nine inches tall and weighed more than 350 pounds when, as a member of the U.S. sports team, he outlifted every Russian contestant in Moscow. He went on to win the title of World Weightlifting Champion, breaking Olympic records in 1955 and 1956. His greatest weightlifting feat happened on June 12, 1957. On top of an especially sturdy table was placed a steel safe and several very heavy pieces of metal. The total weight was more than that of an average car. Before the eyes of an anxious crowd, Paul positioned himself under the table. With sweat pouring down and muscles bulging. Paul pushed his back against the underside of the table. At first nothing happened. Then slowly but surely the table legs left the floor. Paul had lifted 6,270 pounds with his back.

## THE FIRST THREE-FOOT, SEVEN-INCH BATTER

In August 1951 Bill Veeck, owner of the St. Louis Browns, signed Eddie Gaedel, a midget, to a one-day contract with the team. Attendance had been low at the games, and Veeck promised the fans "a festival of surprises" at the August 19 game. When Eddie entered the game as a pinch hitter, the umpires objected, until they were shown his contract. Eddie was ordered by Veeck not to swing at a ball. Bob Cain, the pitcher, sent four high balls over the plate. Eddie walked to first base, bowing to the loudly cheering crowd.

(1 of 2)

# THE FIRST MAJOR LEAGUE PLAYER TO BECOME A MOVIE STAR

Kevin Connors was an all-around athlete. His natural ability earned him a college scholarship. World War II intervened, and Kevin enlisted to serve as a tank warfare instructor. After discharge from the army he joined the Boston Celtics basketball team but left the team when he got an offer to play with the Brooklyn Dodgers in 1949. In 1951 he played for the Chicago Cubs. A year later, what should have been a disappointment turned out to be good fortune. Kevin was sent by the Cubs to play in their farm team, the Los Angeles Angels. There he was spotted by a movie casting director and offered a part in the movie *Pat and Mike,* starring Spencer Tracy and Katherine Hepburn. More movie roles followed and led to the starring role in the popular television series *The Rifleman.* Fans knew him as Chuck Connors. In 1991 he was inducted into the Western Performers Hall of Fame.

# THE FIRST BAT BOY TO PLAY ON A PROFESSIONAL TEAM

Joe Reliford was a lucky 10-year-old. He was hired as a bat boy for the Fitzgerald Pioneers. For two years he traveled with the team. He became a favorite of the players, who taught him to bat and field a ball. On July 19, 1952, the Pioneers were losing 13–0. The disgusted fans began chanting, "Send in the bat boy." Charlie Ridgeway, the manager, figured things couldn't get any worse, so he sent Joel in to pinch hit for another batter. Joel hit a grounder and almost made it in time to first base. As a fielder, Joel caught a long fly ball, preventing a home run. Although the Pioneers lost the game, Joel was a winner as he grinned at the loud cheers of the fans.

# THE FIRST MAJOR LEAGUE ONE-ARMED PLAYER

Six-year-old Peter Wyshner lost his right arm in a train accident, but the handicap did not keep him from playing baseball. He played all through his youth and in his late teens he bet the manager of the Brooklyn Bushwicks that he could be a plus to the team. He changed his name to Pete Gray, so the fans could remember it, and won his bet. Fans filled the stands to see him play, and in 1944 he was voted the most valuable player in the Southern Association. He was signed to a Major League contract with the St. Louis Browns. Pete worried that he was hired for his ability to draw fans rather than his playing ability. Those fears were put to rest when he was sent in to play against the New York Yankees. Using a special glove, he would catch the ball, roll the glove under his right arm, and throw the ball with his left hand. In the Brown–Yankees game he got four hits, scored two runs, and made nine plays in the outfield. Pete Gray showed everyone he belonged on a Major League team.

# RESEARCH REPORT: FAMOUS FIRST FACTS

Check out the library reference section for *Famous First Facts* by Joseph Kane. Find 10 that you think are the funniest and most unusual. **Complete this pattern** with the information you find. **Standards** I-A, E; II-D; III-B, D

A man named Joe got into the act,
When he searched and searched for a famous first fact.
In looking them over, sakes alive!
Here, I think, are the strangest five.

_____

_____

_____

_____

_____

First in politics, travel, and then,
Firsts for women and firsts for men,
First on land and first in space,
I've chosen five more for the funniest first place.

_____

_____

_____

_____

_____

Now Joe was not a man to brag
But famous first facts weren't easy to snag
Funny and strange, you've chosen a few
Add one from your life that's a First for YOU!

_____

_____

_____

_____

# DESPITE A HANDICAP

These people achieved fame in their fields despite a handicap. **Standards** I-A, B, C; II-D, E, F, G; III-E, F, G

Ludwig van Beethoven wrote his greatest music after becoming deaf.

Helen Keller wrote, lectured, and inspired millions although deaf and blind.

Pete Gray was a Major League pitcher with one arm.

Franklin Delano Roosevelt, president of the United States, was paralyzed from the waist down.

Louis Braille, inventor the Braille system that enabled the blind to read, was himself blind.

Stephen Hawking, discoverer of black holes, suffered from a disease that confined him to a wheel chair.

## An A–Z Report: Louis Braille, 1809–1852

A child

B orn in France, 1809

C arried on conversations at age three

D ealt an eye injury in his father's shop

E very medical help sought

F ruitless in saving his sight

G one completely in both eyes

H e learned to play the cello

I nterested in piano as well

J oined others in the local school

K ept listening and e

L earned well enough to be at the top of his class

M oved to Paris in 1819

N ew student at the National Institute for the Blind

O ver time became a teacher

P resented with a system of raised dots

Q uestioned their value at first

R estructured to a six dot code, now

S ightless people could read

T reatises published at age 20

U nacceptable to many

V ictory was his despite criticism

W ith variations for musical notation

X ceptional man who helped many

Y oung age to die at 43

Z ealous in his desire to help others

# RESEARCH REPORT: THE A–Z REPORT

**Choose** a handicapped person who achieved fame in his or her field and **summarize** his or her life in 26 phrases or sentences, A–Z. See the example given on page 73 for Louis Braille.
**Standards** I-A, B, C; II-D, E, F, G; III-E, F, G

A  _____

B  _____

C  _____

D  _____

E  _____

F  _____

G  _____

H  _____

I  _____

J  _____

K  _____

L  _____

M  _____

N  _____

O  _____

P  _____

Q  _____

R  _____

S  _____

T  _____

U  _____

V  _____

W  _____

X  _____

Y  _____

Z  _____

# Resources:
# People Who Were First

---

*Amelia Earhart: Free in the Skies,* by Robert Burleigh. Silver Whistle, 2003.

Story of the first woman to fly across the Atlantic Ocean.

*Condoleezza Rice: Being the Best,* by Mary Wade. Millbrook, 2003.

The story of the first black woman to become secretary of state.

*Daring Nellie Bly,* by Bonnie Christensen. Knopf, 2003.

The woman reporter who introduced investigative reporting.

*Elizabeth Blackwell: Girl Doctor,* by Joanne Henry. Simon & Schuster, 1996.

Admitted to medical school as a joke, Elizabeth graduated first in her class to become the nation's first woman doctor.

*Glorious Flight,* by Alice Provensen. Viking, 1983.

The flight attempts of Louis Bleriot.

*Kate Shelley: Bound for Legend,* by Robert San Souci. Dial, 1995.

A young girl risks her life to warn an approaching train that a bridge has collapsed.

*Lives of Extraordinary Women,* by Kathleen Krull. Harcourt, 2003.

Women who were first in many fields.

*More Strange But True Sports Stories,* by Howard Liss.Random House, 1981.

Those who were first in many different sports, from baseball to tennis.

*Picture Book of Louis Braille,* by David Adlerr. Holiday House, 1997.

Story of the 15-year-old who gave the blind a way to read.

*Story of Clara Barton,* by Rachel Koestler-Grack. Chelsea House, 2004.

Easy-to-read biography of the founder of the American Red Cross.

*Strange But True Baseball Stories,* by Furman Bisher. Scholastic, 1966.

Amusing, amazing, and offbeat moments in baseball history.

*Susan B. Anthony: Fighter for Women's Rights,* by Deborah Hopkinson. Aladdin, 2005.

The woman and her fight for equality for women.

*Woman for President: The Story of Victoria Woodhull.* by Kathleen Krull. Walker, 2004.

The little-known account of the first woman to run for president of the United States.

# Part Seven

# Unbelievable People

On January 26, 1972, an explosion sent a DC9 flying at 33,000 feet crashing to the ground. Vesna Vulovic, the flight attendant, survived the crash!

A man from Poona, India, named Chillal had five fingernails on his left hand with a combined length of more than 20 feet.

When Robert Wadlow passed away in 1940 he was the tallest man in the world, at eight feet, eleven inches. His shoe size was 37AA.

Russian Nickolai Sutyagin built a log cabin 13 floors high. He wanted to impress his neighbors.

Merhan Karimi Nasseri was stuck in the Charles de Gaulle Airport for 14 years.

Louis Hamburger, of Baltimore, attracted metal objects, which would attach and dangle from his hands

During the Korean War, Ferdinand Demara performed 19 successful operations as a ship's doctor. He had no medical training.

# UNBELIEVABLE WALKERS

## SHANKS MARE WILL GET YOU THERE

Using his own two feet for transportation, Scottish Captain Allardyce Barklay accepted a bet to walk 1,000 miles in 1,000 hours regardless of weather. There were to be no breaks in the thousand-hour count. Barklay began his walk on June 1, 1809. He walked the half mile to the town of Newcastle, then turned around and walked home. As the hours and the miles grew, Barklay had blisters on his feet and cramps in his legs but kept going. Interest among the towns-folk grew, and more and more bets were made. Barklay's brother made sure the route was lit up at night to prevent the walker being attacked by those who bet he would lose. On July 12 the walker completed the final mile 45 minutes ahead of schedule.

## ED WESTON WALKED FROM NEW YORK TO CALIFORNIA

Edward Payson Weston was a walker! He walked the 478 miles from Boston to Washington, D.C., in 10 days to see the inauguration of Abraham Lincoln. He made the trip, eating as he walked, despite heavy snows and driving rains. A few years later he won a $10,000 bet by walking from Portland, Maine, to Chicago in 26 days. His longest walk took place in 1909, when he was 70 years old. He walked from New York to Sanm Francisco (3,895 miles).

## A WALK IN THE WOODS

Roy C. Sullivan was a U.S. park ranger who was struck by lightning seven times between 1942 and 1983 and lived to tell about it. He was on duty in 1942 in a lookout tower when lightning struck. It burned his big toenail off. Two more strikes hit him in 1969 and 1979. The first knocked him out and the second burned his left shoulder. Staying indoors didn't help. He was in the ranger office in 1972 when lightning struck and set his hair on fire. One year later lightning set his regrown hair on fire again. One moment he was driving his truck, and the next he was thrown out on the road with burned legs. Strike number six happened when Roy was inspecting campsites and the last, in 1977, put him in the hospital with burns on his torso. Not only does no one else hold this record, but it is a sure thing that no one wants to.

# RESEARCH REPORT: THE YOUNGEST RUNNER

Five-year-old "Marathon Boy," Buddha of India ran 40 miles in seven hours and two minutes without stopping. He made the Indian *Book of World Records.* However, when he tried to enter a 300-mile walking marathon he was stopped from participating by health authorities, who felt the distance would be a danger to the boy's health.

## A STRANGE PLACE FOR A MARATHON

Marathon runners who wanted a real challenge in 2002 signed up for a walking marathon at the South Pole. Runners faced ice, snow (like walking in mud), and a 9-000-foot elevation, in temperatures that hovered around zero. The entry fee was $25,000. Not too many folks signed up.

## TRAINING FOR A WALKING MARATHON

Begin with a 10- to 15-minute warm up, and end with 5- to 10-minute cool down

One day a week, practice speed by doing short intervals at a fast pace.

One day go at a faster pace (Tempo walk). A Tempo is a steady, fast workout.

One long distance day at a moderate pace.

One day off each week: You are stressing your body, so take a day of rest each week.

Stretching: After you work out you must also spend time stretching.

**Find out about** a walking marathon in your area. **Standards** III-D, E

Date _____

Starting Point _____

Distance _____

Qualifications _____

_____

Prizes _____

Walking trivia quiz game: who wants to be a walking wizard?

walking.about.com/cs/cardsandclipart/a/quizwizard.htm: Take the walking trivia quiz and find out how you would do. (There are no prizes.)

# RESEARCH REPORT: EXERCISE OR MEDITATION?

Both Jack LaLanne and Ashrita Furman are record holders. At age 60 Jack swam from Alcatraz Island to Fisherman's Wharf in San Francisco, shackled, handcuffed, and towing a 1,000-pound boat. At age 65 he towed 10 boats over a mile in less than an hour. Seventy-seven people were on board. Jack attributes his strength and fitness to daily exercise; in fact, his belief in exercise has led him to be called the "Father of Fitness."

Ashrita Furman currently holds 14 records in the *Guinness Book of World Records*. He walked 81 miles with a milk bottle on his head; made 130,000 rope jumps in 24 hours; did 27,000 jumping jacks without stopping; and made the fastest pogo stick ascent of Canada's CN Tower, in 57 minutes and 51 seconds, among other records. Ashrita attributes his fitness to meditation. By meditating he claims he overcomes any physical pain in attempting a record.

## Propaganda and Exercise Machines

Examine at least three television commercials or print advertisements for exercise machines. List below three machines and the number of each propaganda technique used to sell each machine. Give a specific example of one technique. **Standards** I-C, D, F, H, I; III-C, D

COMMON PROPAGANDA TECHNIQUES ARE:

1. WIDE GENERALIZATIONS: suggest that something applies to all people
2. FALSE ANALOGIES: compare things that cannot be truthfully compared
3. BANDWAGON DEVICES: "Everyone is doing it."
4. SNOB APPEAL: use of celebrities in ads
5. REPETITION: repeating slogans over and over
6. APPEALING TO FEAR: Dire consequences will happen if the product is not used, or the product assures safety above the norm.
7. TESTIMONIALS: endorsement by a product user
8. HALF TRUTHS: Omit important facts
9. EGO TRIPS: The product will make you the envy of friends or neighbors.

1. Machine _____

   Techniques Used _____

   Example _____

2. Machine _____

   Techniques Used _____

   Example _____

3. Machine _____

   Techniques Used _____

   Example _____

# CREATIVE WRITING: MAGNETIC PEOPLE

There are many documented cases of people who, strangely enough, attract metal objects. Their bodies act like a magnet.

In 1889, Frank McKinstry had to keep moving when he went outside. If he stopped his legs would become attached to the ground, and another person would have to lift his legs to get him going again. Frank lived in the small town of Joplin, Missouri.

In 1997 Miroslaw Magola's ability to attract metal objects was studied at the Max Planck Institute in Germany. Miroslaw demonstrated his ability to pick up a metal up from the floor and hold it in the air without touching it. Small metal objects would cling to any part of his body.

In 1890 young Louis Hamburger could pick up heavy metal objects by touching them. He could make iron filings move up and down the inside of a jar by moving his hand up and down on the outside of the jar.

For 40 years Mrs. Grace Charlesworth was shocked by touching metal objects in her home. When she walked through a room, electric sparks shot up the walls.

Suppose you had the combined abilities of the people described above. **List three positive ways and one negative way** you could use these abilities. **Standards** I-C, H; II-A

If I were a magnetic person:

I could _____

_____

and _____

_____

and _____

_____

But I would not _____

_____

Because that would do harm to _____

# DICTIONARY SKILLS: WOLF GIRLS

It was a dark night in October 1920. The Rev. Singh of Midnapore, India, kept watch with the village people over a large ant hill. As they watched, wolves emerged. Following the wolves were two young girls, one about eight years old and the other about two. The girls snarled, bit with sharp pointed teeth, and fought more fiercely than the wolves when the villagers struggled to capture them. Singh and his wife took the girls home but found it nearly impossible to humanize them. They ran on all fours, refused to stand upright, ate only meat, slept during the day, and moved about only at night. Amala, the younger girl, survived only a year in captivity. Kamala, after nine years, adapted to most human ways but still refused to eat anything but milk and meat. The poor diet brought about her death in 1929.

## About Wolves

1. Long legs, large feet, and a deep chest enable the wolf to travel great distances.
2. Packs of six to ten are most common. Each pack has a leader. The weak are left to die.
3. Wolves communicate through body and tail positions and facial expressions.
4. The young born in a den or burrow and are full grown within six months.
5. Wolves defend their territory against other wolves. They live in the wild up to 13 years.
6. Wolves are meat eaters. They move and hunt mostly at night and can run up to 37 mph.

**Write four sentences** about wolves using a pair of homonyms below in each sentence. Check meanings in the dictionary. **Standards** I-A, E; II-D, G, I

| | | | |
|---|---|---|---|
| weak | wade | waive | ware |
| week | weighed | wave | where |
| we'll | wail | wear | weather |
| wheel | whale | where | whether |
| wood | waist | wait | wet |
| would | waste | weight | whet |

**Example:** In one **week** two **weak** wolves were found wandering in the forest.

1. _____

_____

2. _____

_____

3. _____

_____

4. _____

_____

# ABOUT MISERS

In creating the character of Ebenezer Scrooge, Charles Dickens might have been writing about two famous British misers, Daniel Dancer (1716–1794) and John Camden Neild (1780–1852). To save money, Daniel's daily food was hard dumplings. His food was always cold because he did not want to spend money to reheat it. He never bathed and wore the same clothes day after day until they became rags. He refused to pay for a doctor for his very ill house-keeper sister, who died without medical help. Afraid of thieves, he hid money everywhere. After his death, searchers found £2,500 in a dung heap.

John Neild doubled the large amount of money he inherited from this father by dressing in rags and sleeping on the floor (so he would not have to buy a bed). He argued over every expense and managed to show up at meal times at the poor cottages of the workers on his estate.

## AN AMERICAN MISER

They called her the "Witch of Wall Street." Her real name was Hetty Green. Her father left her $1 million when he died. Hetty was 30 years old and spent the rest of her life holding on to her money. She never heated food because heat cost money. She wore the same black dress day after day, refusing to have it washed. She married only to keep her relatives from inheriting her money. When her son was injured in a accident, she dressed him in rags and took him to the hospital charity ward. When she was recognized, she refused to pay for his treatment. She took him home, and her treatment of his injury caused him to lose his leg. She died in 1916 of a stroke while in a violent argument over the price of milk. Her two children enjoyed spending the millions of dollars she left.

# RESEARCH REPORT: THE ACROSTIC

Below you will see Hetty Green's life described by using the letters of her name for each sentence or phrase. This is called an acrostic.

**Research the life** of Charles Dickens. Describe his life using the acrostic. **Standards** I-B, E; II-A, D, E; III-B, C, D

Charles Dickens was the creator of Ebenezer Scrooge, the world's most famous literary miser.

**H** er goal was to hoard money.

**E** very expense was questioned.

**T** attered clothes did not bother her.

**T** o prevent relatives from inheriting, she got married.

**Y** earning for more riches consumed her.

**G** reed was her watchword.

**R** ags for her son when he was injured.

**E** ntered the charity hospital but turned away.

**E** fforts to care for him herself cost the child his leg.

**N** ever spent a penny she did not have to.

C _____

H _____

A _____

R _____

L _____

E _____

S _____

D _____

I _____

C _____

K _____

E _____

N _____

S _____

# RESEARCH REPORT: AHEAD OF HIS TIME

In 1793, 81-year-old Lord Rokeby of Great Britain had estates covering thousands of acres. His father and grandfather before him were overseers to tenant farmers who grew a variety of crops. The crops were sold and the proceeds helped to run the estate. His neighbors thought Lord Rokeby quite strange, if not a bit balmy. He was a fresh air lover and took long, long walks in the countryside. He refused to grow crops on his land, and his vast estate became a wildlife refuge for all kinds of birds and animals. He believed that sugar, coffee, and alcohol were bad for health and refused to touch them, Instead, he drank water, lots and lots of water. At a time when few people bathed, he installed a special house with a bathtub and frequently went swimming in the sea. At the time Lord Rokeby lived, 40 was considered a ripe old age. Lord Rokeby died in 1801 at the age of 88.

**Take a healthy eating poll**. Interview six classmates about how each prefers his or her food cooked. Count the checks under each choice. **Standards** III-E, G

| Food | Steamed | Baked | Broiled | Fried |
|---|---|---|---|---|
| Hamburger | | | | |
| Potatoes | | | | |
| Chicken | | | | |
| Corn | | | | |
| Apples | | | | |

1. Which method of food preparation is the least healthy?

    _____

2. The method of food preparation most preferred by those polled is

    _____

3. In general, the group polled has (circle one):   healthy   unhealthy   eating habits.

    _____

# RESEARCH REPORT: THE $65 MILLION PANTS

Judge Roy L. Pearson Jr. would be at the top of almost anyone's list for unbelievable things people do. It seems that in May 2005 Judge Pearson took several suits to be cleaned to Custom Cleaners in Washington, D.C. When he requested one of the suits two days later, the pants were missing. Pearson then demanded that the cleaners pay him $1,000, the full price of the suit. The cleaners refused and a week later told Pearson they had found the pants. The Judge said the pants were not his and brought suit against the cleaners for $65 MILLION. This included $.5 million for attorneys' fees, $2 million for "mental distress," and $15,000 to rent a car every weekend to drive to a different dry cleaning service. The remaining millions would be used to help other dissatisfied D.C. consumers sue businesses.

The owners of the cleaning business, South Korean immigrants Jin Nam Chung and his wife, Soo Chung, offered to pay Pearson $12,000 to settle the lawsuit. Pearson rejected the offer

On June 25, 2007, the two-week trial ended. Judge Judith Bartnoff ruled in favor of the dry cleaners and awarded them court costs of $1,000. The Chungs were still left with thousands of dollars in attorneys' fees. Help with these fees came from people all over the country, who sent donations to the Chungs because they were so outraged at Pearson's ridiculous lawsuit. "Who," cried the outraged citizens," would believe that any pair of pants was worth $65 million?" Pearson appealed the verdict.

**Research Activity:** Follow the pattern of steps that starts with the planting of the seeds and ends with the finished cotton garment. Research the steps, from shearing the sheep to cutting and sewing a wool suit. **Standards** I-B, E; II-A, D, E; III-B, C, D

| I Wonder Why They . . . | I Wonder Why They |
|---|---|
| Prepare the soil | |
| Plant the seeds | |
| Cultivate the earth | |
| Spray the crops | |
| Pick the cotton | |
| Remove the fibers | |
| Bale the lint | |
| Truck the bales | |
| Clean the cotton | |
| Spin the thread | |
| Weave the yarn | |
| Dye the cloth | |
| Cut and sew | |
| When I could wear | |
| WOOL INSTEAD! | |

# RESEARCH REPORT: THE MAN WITHOUT A COUNTRY

Merhan Nasseri was expelled from his country, Iran, for taking part in protests against the government. He was given refugee status in Belgium in 1981. Rather than staying in Belgium Nasseri decided to travel to England. Unfortunately his papers and all of his belongings were stolen in France, and with no passport the English authorities sent him back to France. When he arrived at Charles de Gaulle Airport the French authorities would not allow him into the country because he had no passport. When the Belgian government was notified they told the French officials that a refugee who leaves the country is not allowed to return. For the next 12 years the Charles de Gaulle Airport became Nasseri's home.

## Research Activity

How can a person born in another country become a citizen of the United States? Check the almanac for the basic requirements and complete the fact/opinion chart. **Standards** I-A, E; II-D; III-B, D

| STATEMENT | FACT | OPINION | PROOF* |
|---|---|---|---|
| The minimum age to apply for citizenship is 18. | | | |
| Children born in the United States of immigrant parents are not U.S. citizens. | | | |
| An applicant must have been a resident of the United States for five or more years. | | | |
| It is not necessary for an applicant to read, write, and speak English. | | | |
| Applicants must demonstrate a knowledge of the Constitution and of U.S. history. | | | |
| Applicants must swear an oath of allegiance to the United States. | | | |
| *For proof write the almanac page number where the information appears. | | | |

# RESEARCH REPORT:
# THE GIRL WHO CHASED FIRE ENGINES

Hilly San Francisco in 1858 proved to be a challenge for fire wagons that were pulled by horses. Some hills were so steep that the men had to pull the fire wagon up a hill with ropes.

One lazy afternoon the fire alarm sounded. Short of men, Knickerbocker Number 5 left the firehouse on its way to a fire on Telegraph Hill. When it came to a very steep hill, there were not enough men on the ropes. Two other fire wagons passed the Knickerbocker. Just then 15-year-old Lillie Hitchcock broke from the group of onlookers. She ran to a vacant place on the rope and began to pull, shouting to the crowd, "Come on, everybody pull and we'll beat 'em." Everybody pulled and the Knickerbocker shot up the hill, arriving at the fire first.

Five years later Lillie became an honorary member of the Knickerbocker Company. She never missed a fire, once leaving a wedding in which she was a bridesmaid when she heard the alarm. She rode on the engine in all the parades, she visited sick firemen, and she sent flowers to the deceased. Her proudest possession was her gold fireman's badge, which she wore at all times.

**Complete the information below** about four other brave women. **Standards** I-A, E; II-D; III-B, D

| WHO | WHAT | WHEN | WHERE | WHY |
|---|---|---|---|---|
| Dolores Huerta | beaten by a mob | 1988 | California | Spoke out for rights of migrant workers |
| Molly Pitcher | | | | |
| Dolley Madison | | | | |
| Molly Brown | | | | |
| Mary Ann Bickerdyke | | | | |

# RESEARCH REPORT: PEOPLE INVENT THE STRANGEST THINGS!

The U.S. Patent Office has issued patents for the following inventions:

Electrified table cloth: Shocks bugs to keep them from crawling on the table.

Hiccup cure: A glass that shocks when you drink from it is supposed to stop hiccups.

Cat exerciser: A laser pointer beam that is moved around so that a cat will chase it and thus get needed exercise.

Transparent shoe: Shoe with a see-through sole to prevent smuggling of jewels or drugs through customs.

Umbrella pillow: A pillow with a retractable umbrella to protect you from the sun.

Pet display: A series of hollow, transparent tubes worn around the neck so that your hamster can crawl around in them.

Tricycle lawnmower: A tricycle with a lawnmower attached.

**Create a limerick** about your favorite inventor. Include at least two facts about the inventor in the limerick. **Standards** I-B, E; II-A, D, E; III-B, C, D

**Example:**

Name: Ada Lovelace
A mathematician indeed
She saw a definite need
In 1843
She invented with glee
A computer that people could read.

Name _____

_____

_____

_____

_____

_____

# Resources:
# Unusual People

*African American Inventors,* by Otha Richard Sullivan. Wiley, 1998.

Twenty-five inventors whose inventions helped change the way we live.

*Andy Warhol: Pop Art Painter,* by Susan Goldman Rubin. Abrams, 206.

His art was so different people called him crazy, yet there was something about it that made the viewer take a second look.

*Barnum Brown: Dinosaur Hunter,* by David Sheldon. Walker, 2006.

He discovered the first nearly complete *Tyrannosaurus rex*!

*The Daring Nellie Bly,* by Bonnie Christensan. Knopf, 2003.

This stunt reporter got herself committed to an asylum to get a scoop and traveled around the world in record time.

*Dizzy,* by Jonah Winter. Arthur A. Levine Books, 2006.

The story of Dizzy Gillespie, who originated a strange new kind of music called bebop.

*Edmund Hillary: First to the Top,* by Dan Elish. Walker, 2006.

The life of the New Zealand explorer who was first to climb to the top of Mount Everest.

*The Fighter Wore a Skirt,* by Nancy Polette. Pieces of Learning, 2005.

Narrative poems about 32 daring American women.

*Firebell Lillie,* by Helen Holdredge. Meredith Press, 1967.

The story of Lillie Hitchcock, mascot of San Francisco firefighters.

*Honky-Tonk Heroes and Hilllbilly Angels,* by Holly George-Warren. Houghton Mifflin, 2006.

Profiles of the pioneers of country western music.

*Ladies First: Forty Daring Women Who Were Second to None,* by Elizabeth Kimmel. National Geographic, 2006.

Women who dared society or their professions to achieve fame in a variety of fields, from the arts to politics.

*Perplexing People,* by Gary Blackwood. Marshall Cavendish, 2006.

Describes people in history who pretended to be someone they were not.

*Snowflake Bentley,* by Jacqueline Briggs Martin. Houghton Mifflin, 1998.

Neighbors thought Wilson Bentley strange. After all, who would spend his whole life studying snowflakes?

*Twenty-Six Men Who Changed the World,* by Cynthia Chinn-Lee. Charlesbridge, 2006.

   Men who were not afraid pushed beyond the boundaries in the arts, sports, science, and government.

*Walking Marathon,* by David McGovern. World Class Publications, 2000.

   A complete guide to marathon walking.

*When I Met the Wolf Girls,* by Deborah Noyes. Houghton Mifflin, 2007.

   Story of two girls raised by wolves and brought to civilization.

# ADULT BOOKS

Baldwin, Gordon. *Strange People and Stranger Customs.* Norton, 1967

Berlitz, Charles, *Strange People and Amazing Stories.* Time Warner, 1990.

Edwards, Frank. *Strange People.* Lyle Stuart, 1986.

Emert, Phyllis. *Mysteries of People and Places.* Tor Books, 1992

Evans, Adelaide. *Strange Peoples and Customs.* Pacific Press, 1921.

Smith, Brandon. *Unusual People, Places and Events.* Authorhouse, 2001.

# Part Eight

# Bits of History

## Wacky History Facts

The first news of the Declaration of Independence was printed in German in a Philadelphia newspaper.

Bartholdi, designer of the Statue of Liberty, used as models his wife's body and his mother's face.

A July 4, 1776, diary entry of King George III of England read: "Nothing of importance happened today."

The first U.S. Army in 1789 had 840 soldiers.

While in the White House, Theodore Roosevelt had three dogs, two cats, a badger, a pony, a macaw, a garter snake, twelve horses, five bears, five guinea pigs, a rooster, an owl, a lizard, a flying squirrel, a lion, a zebra, a hyena, and two kangaroo rats.

# CONCLUSION PAPER: DID COLUMBUS REALLY DISCOVER AMERICA? (1492)

Most schoolchildren can recite this rhyme about the man who supposedly discovered America:

Columbus sailed the ocean blue
In fourteen hundred ninety-two

**Examine these facts** and draw your own conclusions.

1.  Diggers in the state of Maine dug up coins from ancient Rome.

2.  In Round Rock, Texas, archaeologists were exploring a 1,200-year-old Indian mound and turned up coins from ancient Rome.

3.  In Oklahoma in 1976 a coin was found with the picture of Nero and dated AD 63.

4.  In Minnesota a large stone was found in 1898 that contained writing telling of a group of Norsemen who explored parts of North America in the 1300s.

5.  In 1886 a sunken ship was found in the bay at Galveston, Texas. It was a Roman ship.

**Draw your own conclusions. Standards** I-B, C, H, I

The evidence above is/is not conclusive enough to show that North America had visitors before Columbus (other than Native Americans) because:

_____

_____

_____

_____

_____

_____

_____

_____

_____

_____

# IMPOSTOR! (1771)

In 1770 Caroline Vernon, a lady-in-waiting to British Queen Charlotte, needed a maid. She hired 16-year-old Sarah Wilson. In her job Sarah spent many days at the palace. She watched the lords and ladies. She watched the queen. She learned much about life at court.

Sad to say, Sarah was a thief. She stole jewels and a dress from the queen's closet. The second time she approached the closet she was caught. In 1771 she was banned from England, put on a ship to the New World, and sold as a slave to Mr. W. Devall.

Sarah soon escaped. Wearing the stolen dress and a ring she had managed to keep, she told everyone she was Princess Susanna, sister of the queen. She said she had been forced to travel to the New World because of a family quarrel.

The more wealthy settlers welcomed her into their homes. They enjoyed her tales of court life and gave her both money and expensive gifts. Sarah was in her glory. Meanwhile Mr. Devall heard about the princess. She sounded like his former slave. He sent someone to investigate. Sarah was brought back to the Devall plantation at gunpoint.

Two years later she again escaped, but Devall gave up the chase. By now Sarah had learned her lesson. No more thieving. No more impersonations. She married a young officer. Both got through the Revolutionary War safely and settled down to a happy married life.

# RESEARCH REPORT: IMPOSTORS

Two of the best known impostors in history were Princess Caribou and Frank Thompson. Both were able to fool those they came into contact with for a considerable length of time. Read about each of these impostors in the encyclopedia or on the Internet.

**Complete the chart below. Standards** II-D, E; III-C, D, E

|  | **Princess Caribou** | **Frank Thompson** |
|---|---|---|
| **Birth/Death** |  |  |
| **Nationality** |  |  |
| **Disguised as** |  |  |
| **Reason for disguise** |  |  |
| **Exposed when** |  |  |
| Which disguise was justified? Why? | | |
| _____ | | |
| _____ | | |
| _____ | | |
| _____ | | |
| _____ | | |
| _____ | | |
| _____ | | |
| _____ | | |

# RESEARCH REPORT:
# THE ALAMO (1836)

Davy Crockett was a legend in his own time. It was said that he had wrestled bears, fought Indians, and saved lots of folks in trouble. He also served three terms as a Congressman. That's why in February 1836 Davy and his friend George Russel headed for Texas. It seemed that the Mexican General, Santa Anna, vowed to expel all the American settlers in Texas. Earlier he had sent an army to fight the settlers and his army was defeated. This made Santa Anna vow revenge! He gathered together an army of 4,000 men and began marching toward the Alamo, where the Texans were waiting. Davy was determined to get there before the general. "A good fighter is always needed," he said. And get there he did, before the 10-day fight began, pitting 182 brave men against Santa Anna's army.

**Good Reading:**

*Inside the Alamo* by Jim Murphy. Delacorte Press, 2003.

*The Alamo* by Dennis Frindell Braden, Benchmark, 2007.

**Read more about** Davy Crockett at the Alamo. Complete the sentences that follow, supporting your statements with factual information. **Standards** I-A, B, E; II-A, C, D, I; III-D, F

**Example:**

Davy Crockett was a ROCK: Though he knew that Santa Anna's army of 4,000 would win, he remained steadfast and fought until his death.

Davy Crockett was a COMPASS _____

_____

Davy Crockett was AN OAK TREE _____

_____

Davy Crockett was a STAR _____

_____

Davy Crockett was a RACEHORSE _____

_____

Davy Crockett was a REAPER _____

_____

Davy Crockett was a FRIEND _____

_____

# RESEARCH REPORT: A FUNERAL FOR A LEG (1837)

Santa Anna was never one to miss an opportunity. In 1833 the president of Mexico was murdered by revolutionary forces. Santa Anna immediately stepped in and declared himself president. He had a reputation for destroying those who opposed him, so no one argued.

As president and general of his troops, he also had low tolerance for rebellion of any kind. When 182 Texas upstarts in a mission called the Alamo declared Texas free from Mexico, Santa Anna decided to teach the upstarts a lesson. He attacked the Alamo with his 4,000-man army and defeated the Texans. With those odds, there was little doubt about the outcome.

However, he did not have long to celebrate his victory. It was followed quickly by his defeat at the hands of Sam Houston at San Jacinto. He was taken prisoner and not released until he signed an agreement to free Texas from Mexico. He returned to Mexico as a defeated general and lost his job as president.

Santa Anna was not one to take defeat easily. In 1837, when the French tried to invade Mexico, Santa Anna led the battle against them. Unfortunately he was shot in the leg. Infection set in and the leg had to be amputated. Santa Anna planned an elaborate funeral, and the leg was buried with full military honors. That got everyone's attention, and he became president of Mexico once more.

Here are two famous Americans who did not have a funeral. Research the mysterious death of Meriwether Lewis or Amelia Earhart. Complete the pattern below.


The death of _____ is a perfect puzzle. Some reporters believe that

_____

_____. Historians disagree. Most believe that

_____

_____. It is quite possible that

_____

_____. But what

really happened is (give your idea) _____

_____

_____.

# CONCLUSION PAPER: FACT OR LEGEND? THE LOST DUTCHMAN MINE (1845)

In the Superstition Mountains of Arizona, so the story goes, there is a gold mine with the richest gold ore ever mined. In 1845 Jacob Walz, an immigrant, arrived on American shores and headed west, planning to get rich by finding a gold mine. For 20 years Jacob searched for riches. Then he met another prospector, Jacob Weiser, and the two saved the life of a wealthy Mexican. In gratitude the man shared a map with them of a gold mine rich in nuggets. Before long, Jacob Walz showed up in Phoenix with an amazing supply of gold nuggets. He never gave away the location of his mine and evaded any pursuers who tried to follow him. Jacob Weiser mysteriously disappeared, and then it was only Walz who showed up in Phoenix from time to time. It is said that he died in 1891 without ever revealing the location of the mine and with a large sack of gold under his bed. Though many have searched, to this day the Lost Dutchman Mine has never been found.

What do you think? **Describe** Jacob Walz by completing each of the following sentences. **Standards** I-B, E; II-A, I, L

If Jacob Walz were an animal he would be a/an _____

because _____

If Jacob Walz were a plant he would be a/an _____

because _____

If Jacob Walz were a song the title would be _____

because _____

If Jacob Walz were a food he would be a/an _____

because _____

If Jacob Walz were a machine he would be a/an _____

because _____

# BITS OF HISTORY FROM THE CIVIL WAR

## THE PETTICOAT THAT SAVED A SCHOOL (1864)

By 1864 Union and Rebel troops had been fighting for three years. Laura Draper, like many other young girls, was sent to the Danville Academy for young ladies early in the war. No one would bother a girls' school in the sleepy Missouri town of Danville. No one, that is, but Bloody Bill Anderson. It was the night of October 14. Laura was alone in her room on the second floor when Anderson and his guerrillas rode into the schoolyard with torches held high and guns blazing. Danville, the town they had just left, was burning to the ground.

Mrs. Robinson, the headmistress, went out to meet the men and to beg them to spare the school. One bushwhacker stepped up and put a pistol to her head. "Keys to the chapel," he ordered. Without waiting for the keys, he kicked open the huge, heavy door. The chapel was empty.

One of the guerrillas looked up and laughed. Others joined in the laughter. Laura had tied her white petticoat to a stick and was waving her flag of truce out the window. To everyone's surprise, the men turned their steeds and rode out of the schoolyard, laughing. The school was saved.

## THE SNOWBALL FIGHT

On March 22, 1864, snow fell heavily on Georgia troops camped on one side of a ravine and on Tennessee troops camped on the other side. The Tennessee troops started snowball fights among themselves. Before long snowballs were thrown across the ravine by the Georgia troops. The Tennessee troops called on Colonel Gordon to mount his horse and lead an attack. The Georgia troops did the same. Before long the "battle" was in full swing. Some men stockpiled snowballs for ammunition, while those with the strongest arms launched the snowballs at the opposing force. Nearly 5,000 soldiers joined in the fray. Finally, the Tennessee troops broke through the Georgia line, chasing the Georgians from the field. For the remainder of the war Colonel Gorden was called "The Snowball Colonel."

# RESEARCH REPORT: THE CIVIL WAR (1861–1865)

**An Event Bio:**

**Topic:** Bombardment of Fort Sumter

**Symbol of:** Union authority

**Four Location Words:** island, harbor, entrance, Charleston

**Five Action Words:** threatened, bombarded, exploded, evacuated, marched

**Caused by:** Confederate demand for a fort in a seceded state

**Valued by:** both the North and South

**Choices made:** Lincoln's decision to send supplies, Confederate decision to bombard the fort before supplies arrived.

**Lacking:** Enough food and supplies to withstand the bombardment

**Major Players:** Union Major Robert Anderson, Confederate authorities

**Simile:** Rubble left was like an abandoned, collapsed mine

**Outcome:** Victory for the South; evacuation of the fort. Aroused and united the North.

**Choose another event** from the Civil War. Follow the pattern above to tell about the event.
**Standards** I-B ,C, D; II-A, G; III-D, G, H

Topic _____

Symbol of: _____

Four Location Words: _____ _____ _____ _____

Five Action Words: _____ _____ _____ _____ _____ _____

Caused by: _____

Valued by: _____

Choices made: _____

_____

Lacking: _____

Major Players: _____

Simile: _____

Outcome: _____

_____

# QUIZ: A CIVIL WAR QUIZ

Circle the letter under **TRUE** if the statement is true. **Circle the letter under FALSE** if the statement is false. Place the circled letters in order on the lines at the bottom of the page. The word you spell is one reason the war was fought. Use the encyclopedia for the information you need. **Standards** I-B, F; III-D, E

|  |  | True | False |
|---|---|---|---|
| 1. | The war began when the Southern troops fired on Fort Sumter. | E | T |
| 2. | The Union Army won the first Battle of Bull Run. | S | M |
| 3. | Fourteen Southern states withdrew from the Union. | W | A |
| 4. | The war was fought over the issue of states' rights. | N | O |
| 5. | Robert E. Lee led the Confederate troops. | C | L |
| 6. | Andrew Johnson was president during the war. | D | I |
| 7. | The South won a number of victories early in the war. | P | E |
| 8. | Jefferson Davis was the president of the Confederacy. | A | G |
| 9. | Sherman's march to the sea destroyed much of Georgia. | T | A |
| 10. | On April 9, 1865, Lee surrendered to General Sherman. | J | I |
| 11. | More soldiers died of disease than of battle wounds. | O | U |
| 12. | The Battle of Gettysburg saw the most casualties. | N | H |

One major issue over which the war was fought was:

___ ___ ___ ___ ___ ___ ___ ___ ___ ___ ___ ___
1    2    3    4    5    6    7    8    9    10   11   12

⚷ Answer Key: Emancipation

# THE WILD WEST:
# WAS SHE REALLY A CALAMITY? (1865)

## CALAMITY JANE, 1852–1903

In 1865 Martha Canary's family made the five-month journey from Independence, Missouri, to Virginia City. Martha's mother died one year later. Her father died in 1867, leaving Martha an orphan at age 15. In the next few years the young girl traveled from Wyoming, to Utah, to Arizona, and back to Wyoming, where she claimed she worked as a scout for General Custer. That, says Martha, is how she got the name Calamity Jane.

In June 1876 Calamity was hired to carry the U.S. Mail between Deadwood and Custer. The 50-mile route wound over the roughest trails in the Black Hills country. Robbers waited along the way. Calamity made the trip day after day without incident. Her reputation as a sharpshooter kept thieves away.

In the spring of 1877, 12 miles out of Deadwood, Calamity spotted a runaway mail coach. John Slaughter, the driver, lay face down in the driver's seat. The horses were running wild. The coach swayed back and forth. Six men were inside the coach. No one would climb outside and stop the horses. The horses slowed as they reached the Whitewood Creek Station, with a raiding party not far behind. Calamity galloped alongside and took the driver's seat. She got the coach with its six passengers safely to Deadwood.

In 1878 a terrible sickness came to Deadwood. Smallpox! Hundreds came down with the high fever and rash that spread on the face, the palms, and the soles of the feet. A few days later terrible sores covered the body and breathing was difficult. Death often followed. Everyone knew smallpox was catching. There were very few women in mining towns. Most miners were men. No one wanted to nurse those who were taken ill. Fear covered Deadwood like a heavy blanket.

One person was not afraid. The rough-talking, hard-riding, sharpshooting Calamity Jane got off her horse and laid aside her pistol to care for the sick. Days turned into weeks as she brought water to the thirsty, washed fevered faces, and comforted the dying. She did not hesitate to wave her gun if a storekeeper refused food for the sick. Whether they were rich or poor, old or young, Calamity cared for those in need. When others gave up or refused to help, Calamity was there. She put her own life in danger for strangers, rescuing many who would have died without her help. Was she really a calamity? You decide.

# RESEARCH REPORT: WOMEN OF THE WILD WEST (1850–1880)

Much has been written about the lawmen and outlaws of the Wild West, but not only were there women outlaws, there were women who brought real civilization to a lawless land. Choose one of the women listed below. **Finish five proverbs** the way she might finish them. See the example for Calamity Jane. **Standards** I-B, C, D; II-A, G; III-D, G, H

|  |  |
|---|---|
| Clara Brown | Annie Oakley |
| Belle Starr | Charlotte Parkhurst |

**Calamity Jane**

**Still waters** need to be tested before taking a team of horses across.

**If the shoe fits**, you haven't ridden long and hard enough to break it in.

**Actions speak louder than** talking about a situation, especially if there is a runaway coach that needs rescuing.

**He who hesitates** taking care of sick folks might find a lot of them dying.

**Haste makes** for a poor shot.

Woman's name _____ Dates _____ to _____

Still waters _____

A penny saved _____

If the shoe fits _____

Actions speak louder _____

He who hesitates _____

Strike while _____

Every cloud has _____

Haste makes _____

Two wrongs don't _____

# HOW WILD WAS THE WILD WEST? (1870S)

In the 1870s Palisade, Nevada, had the reputation of being one of the wildest towns in the Wild West. For a number of years it had been a watering stop for trains of the Central Pacific Railroad. It was a sleepy town, with few people, no crime, and no sheriff. Then gold was discovered in nearby Eureka and news came that a new railroad line would be built to transport the ore shipments and supplies and bring passengers from the East.

Restaurants and saloons sprang up to take care of the travelers. However, when passengers got off the train all they saw was a sleepy town. They had come to see the Wild West and were disappointed that Palisade was not at all wild. Then a conductor on the railroad made a suggestion. The citizens of Palisade thought it was a great idea.

When passengers disembarked from the next train, they were startled to hear a shout from a rough-looking cowboy. "There you are, you low-down pole cat. I'm gonna kill you." The cowboy pulled out his gun and fired away. The victim hit the dirt and was picked up and carried to the local saloon by the citizens. The train's passengers screamed and scattered and had quite a tale to tell when they reached their final destination. Before long Palisade, Nevada, was known as the roughest town in the West.

The citizens got so good at their play-acting that they varied the scenario by staging an occasional bank robbery. When the railroad eventually ceased operations, Palisade had never had a serious crime or the need for a sheriff.

# RESEARCH REPORT: WHICH TOWN WAS THE WILDEST? (1870S)

**Complete the information** for Tombstone and compare it with Dodge City. **Standards** I-A, B, F, I; II-D, F

|  | Dodge City | Tombstone |
|---|---|---|
| Founded | 1872 | |
| Industry | Buffalo hides/cattle | |
| Railroad stop | yes | |
| Stores | grocery/hardware saloon/barber blacksmith | |
| Lawmen | Bat Masterson Wyatt Earp | |
| Citizens | Buffalo hunters/cattlemen Population 1,200 | |
| Laws | No guns allowed north of railroad tracks. South side "wide open" | |

The wildest town was _____ because

_____

_____ .

# LITERARY DESCRIPTION: WILD WEST TOWNS (1870S)

**Follow the model** given for Dodge City to describe the colors and sounds of Tombstone. **Standards** I-A, B, E; II-A, C, D, I; III-D, F

**I am** Dodge City in 1878
**I am the sound of**
Pounding hammers on weather-beaten boards

Echoes of gunshots from south of the railroad tracks

The chatter of 1,200 citizens

The creaking of wagon wheels hauling weary travelers from the East

The grinding of buffalo bones into fertilizer selling for $6 a ton

The lowing of five million cattle driven up the western branch of the Chisholm Trail.

**My colors are**

The oozing brown mud of streets battere by heavy rain

The shining rails of the Atchison, Topeka & Santa Fe

The red caboose lanterns of the train masters

The massive gray piles of stinking buffalo hides

The silver stars of law and order worn by Bat Masterson, Wyatt Earp, and Charlie Bassett

**I am** Tombstone in 1878
**I am the sound of**

_____
_____
_____
_____
_____
_____
_____
_____
_____
_____
_____

**My colors are**

_____
_____
_____
_____
_____
_____
_____
_____
_____
_____

# ONE-EYED CHARLIE, 1812–1879

Driving a stagecoach out West was no easy task. The narrow mountain roads had thousand-foot drops with barely enough room to make a curve. Wild hogs spooked the horses and sent more than one coach plummeting down a mountain. Charlie Parkhurst drove the western trails for 50 years without an accident.

In 1849 Charlie was driving a team on the straight and narrow when Pete, the lead horse, shied. Charlie climbed down to calm the horse and came eye to eye with a three-foot rattlesnake, rattles shaking like a marimba band. A frightened Pete reared up. One sharp hoof came down, hitting Charlie in the face. The snake took off, but the rough-faced driver lost sight in one eye. The accident didn't stop Charlie from driving. Passengers soon got used to the fierce looking, one-eyed driver they called One-Eyed Charlie.

In the Wild West, Charlie and the other drivers kept a sharp eye out for outlaws. The stagecoaches carried mail and gold as well as people. On one trip Sugarfoot and his gang pulled Charlie's coach to a halt and got the gold. The next time they stopped Charlie they got a backside full of buckshot. Charlie was never robbed again.

By 1869 railroads crossed the country. Passengers chose the faster, safer trains. No one wanted stagecoaches. After driving in all kinds of weather, Charlie's hands were crippled with rheumatism. It was time to hang up the reins. For 10 years Charlie lived alone, running a stage station, raising a few cattle and chickens, and hauling small loads of freight. On December 29, 1879, Charlie died in a ramshackle cabin on Bear Creek.

The Wild West knew a lot of rough, tough stagecoach drivers. How, then, was Charlie Parkhurst different? When it was time to dress the body for the funeral, the undertaker was astounded to discover that Charlie was a woman! Her real name was Charlotte Parkhurst, a secret she kept for more than half a century!

# RESEARCH REPORT: FIRST WOMAN TO VOTE (1868)

Charlie Parkhurst drove a stagecoach in the old West for 50 years and it was not until after her death it was discovered that Charlie was a woman. In fact, in the election of 1868, Charlie lined up to vote with the other men (since women were not allowed to vote) and became the first woman to vote in the state of California.

It took the efforts of these and many other women to convince Congress that women should have the right to vote. However, it was not until 1920 that the 19th Amendment was passed giving women this right. Research the life and accomplishments of one of the women listed below.

**Follow the pattern** given for Charlotte Parkhurst to report on the woman you choose. **Standards** I-A, B, E; II-A, C, D, I; III-D, F

| | |
|---|---|
| Victoria Woodhull | Lucretia Mott |
| Elizabeth Cady Stanton | Lucy Stone |
| Susan B. Anthony | |

**Charlotte Parkhurst**
**I am** a stagecoach driver
**I wonder** if I can keep my secret forever

**I hear** the pounding of horses' hooves in my sleep
**I see** tough and winding trails

**I want** to deliver my passengers safely

**I pretend** I am a man

**I touch** the reins with experienced hands

**I cry** never, showing no weakness

**I say** a woman can do any job a man can do
**I try** to avoid robbers but

**I give** as good as I get.

**I am** Charlotte Parkhurst.

**Name** _____
**I am** a suffragette
**I wonder** _____
_____
**I hear** _____
_____
**I see** _____
_____
**I want** _____
_____
**I pretend** _____
_____
**I touch** _____
_____
**I cry** _____
_____
**I say** _____
_____
**I try** _____
_____
**I give** _____
_____
**I am (name)** _____
_____

# RESEARCH REPORT: STAGECOACH ROBBERS

One-eyed Charlie was lucky not to run into the stagecoach robbers Black Bart or Jesse James. Both of them graduated from robbing stagecoaches to robbing trains. Yet many Missourians consider Jesse James to be a modern-day Robin Hood who took from the rich and gave to the poor.

**Read about the life of Jesse James.** Decide if he was an outlaw or a hero. Write about his life using eight couplets. See the example for Black Bart. **Standards** I-A, B, E; II-A, C, D, I; III-D, F

Black Bart played a lot of roles

Real name was Charles Boles


Fought in the War in sixty-one

Headed West when the war was done.


Took to robbing late in life

Used a gun and not a knife


Stagecoaches met a sorry fate

Black Bart robbed all 28


Passengers were warned to stay

Kerchief dropped in getaway


Detective found it in the dark

Traced it through a laundry mark


Realized Bart's greatest fears

Arrested and he got four years


After that no longer feared

Black Bart simply disappeared

# COMBINING HISTORY AND CREATIVE WRITING

**The Beat of America**

EVENT: The End of the Buffalo

Refrain:
Buffalo roaming
Thousands in the distance
Over Western plains
Prairie grass subsistence
CLATTER-CLATTER-BAM-BAM-THUD
CLATTER-CLATTER-BAM-BAM-THUD

Event One
Thousands of buffalo
Echoing refrains
Herds moving westward
Across the western plains

Event Two
Mud-colored giants roaming free
Native Americans buffalo kill
For food and life's necessities
Not for sport or thrill

Event Three
White man came, took the West
Buffalo in each rifle sight
Herds shrink and disappear
Buffalo day has turned to night.

Refrain:
Buffalo gone
No subsistence
Ghostly refrains
Out in the distance
CLATTER-CLATTER-BAM-BAM-THUD
CLATTER-CLATTER-BAM-BAM-THUD

# THE BEAT OF AMERICA

1. Event in history _____

2. Break the event into three parts.

A. _____

B. _____

C. _____

3. Write a beat that is appropriate to the subject. _____

_____

4. Compose a refrain and three verses to describe the event.

| Refrain | Event Three |
|---|---|
| _____ | _____ |
| _____ | _____ |
| _____ | _____ |
| _____ | _____ |
| **Event One** | **Refrain** |
| _____ | _____ |
| _____ | _____ |
| _____ | _____ |
| _____ | _____ |
| **Event Two** | |
| _____ | |
| _____ | |
| _____ | |
| _____ | |

# RESEARCH REPORT:
# IT WASN'T MRS. O'LEARY'S COW! (1871)

Poor Mrs. O'Leary's cow. For years the cow has been blamed for starting the Great Chicago Fire of 1871. It was the disaster that should not have happened. Most of the buildings in Chicago were constructed of wood. For weeks there had been no rain, and the wooden buildings were kindling waiting for the blaze that started in a shed behind the O'Leary house at 137 DeKoven Street. No one thought much of the small blaze when it began. While neighbors formed a fire brigade to save the O'Leary house, they also alerted the fire department. The man on duty thought the smoke was from an earlier fire and did not sound the alarm until much later, when it dawned on him that it was a new fire. Firefighters were slow to respond. They were worn out from fighting a large fire the day before. Strong winds fanned the flames and sent sparks igniting one building after another. The waterworks were destroyed, leaving no way to fight the out-of-control flames. Most of Chicago burned to the ground.

As to the cow . . . there was no cow. Twenty-two years after the fire, a reporter for the *Chicago Republican* admitted that he had made up the cow story. He thought it would make good reading!

**Read more about** the Chicago Fire of 1871. Imagine you had a bird's-eye view of the fire. Use the pattern below to tell what you would see. **Standards** I-A, B, E; II-A, C, D, I; III-D, F

Beware, beware of the fire out there

Hungry flames licking water-starved buildings

_____

_____

_____

_____

_____

_____

_____

_____

So beware!

Use the same pattern to report on another disaster in history.

See a list of disasters on page 119.

# RESEARCH REPORT: ARTIFACTS (1840–1890)

## A STUFFED BIRD

Visitors to the rare book department of the Free Library of Philadelphia might pass by a stuffed bird without knowing what they are seeing. The bird's name is Grip. It belonged to Charles Dickens and was a minor character in his mystery series, *Barnaby Rudge.* When Edgar Allan Poe (1809–1849) read the mystery series he felt that Grip was indeed an unusual bird. After all, how many folks have a raven for a pet? Poe thought Grip should have had a much bigger role in the mystery series. Determined that Grip would be remembered for all time, Poe featured the bird in his famous poem, *The Raven.* Little do readers of the poem know that the raven in the poem was a real bird.

## A BUCKET OF TEETH

Imagine a dentist who can pull 357 teeth on one day! This was Edgar R. R. "Painless" Parker. If you visit Temple University's dental museum, you can see a bucket filled with thousands of teeth pulled by Painless Parker, He was never seen without his top hat and tooth necklace. In the late 1800s he traveled up and down the West Coast, spending part of his time putting on a show and the rest pulling teeth. In time, he became the wealthiest dentist in the United States.

**Visit a museum or your local historical society.** Take along your camera. Photograph unusual artifacts and create a "What Is This Thing?" book. Show the photograph on one page. Give your reader three choices of what it might be. On the next page name and describe the artifacts. **Standards** II-C, D; III-D, E, H

**Example**

| What Is This Thing? | ALICE ROOSEVELT'S DOLL |
|---|---|
| 1. A 19th-century toy? <br><br> 2. Alice Roosevelt's doll? <br><br> 3. A Sesame Street puppet?  | Alice, the daughter of President Theodore Roosevelt, was a tomboy. Her dolls were puppets. She loved putting on puppet shows. She laughed when sometimes the puppets' lines were a bit shocking to her parents. |

For an excellent model, see *What Is This Thing?* by Nancy Polette (Pieces of Learning, 2007).

# WORLD WAR I (1917)

## STUBBY: HERO OF 17 BATTLES

Stubby wasn't old enough to enlist in the army when the United States entered World War I in 1917. This did not keep Stubby from serving. He managed to hide in a large overcoat, and friends smuggled him aboard the troop ship SS *Minnesota*. Little did Stubby guess that he was to take part in seventeen battles and become a hero.

In his first battle Stubby was gassed and was sent back to the field hospital for treatment. When he returned to the front lines he was sensitive to the smell of gas and was able to warn the men of a gas attack, giving them time to put on their gas masks. Stubby's hearing was also much better than that of his comrades. He heard the high whine of the buzz bomb before the other troops. Again, his warning allowed them to take shelter before the bomb hit.

At the Argonne Stubby flushed a German spy out of hiding. Alone, he kept the German pinned down until soldiers arrived to take the spy into custody. He managed to confiscate the German's Iron Cross and kept it for months.

General Blackjack Pershing, supreme commander of the American forces, pinned a gold hero's medal on Stubby. He was written about in newspapers all over the country. He became a lifetime member of the American Legion. He attended every American Legion convention and marched in every Legion parade. He met and shook the hands of three presidents, Wilson, Harding, and Coolidge.

When the time came for Stubby to retire, the YMCA offered him three bones a day and a home for the rest of his life. They were proud to have Stubby the dog as one of their permanent residents!

# MAIN IDEA: STUBBY, HERO OF 17 BATTLES

These sentence strips represent the main ideas of the article about Stubby. **Cut them out and place them in the correct order.**

| |
|---|
| 1. A gassing made Stubby sensitive to gas. |
| 2. The United States entered World War I in 1917. |
| 3. Stubby became a life member of the American Legion. |
| 4. Stubby pinned down a German spy until help came. |
| 5. The YMCA became Stubby's permanent home. |
| 6. Stubby warned troops about gas and bomb attacks. |
| 7. Stubby was a stowaway on a troop ship. |
| 8. General Pershing awarded Stubby a gold medal. |

✂ **Answer Key:** 2, 7, 1, 6, 4, 8, 3, 5

# RESEARCH REPORT: THE GREAT MOLASSES DISASTER OF 1919

The giant storage tank of Purity Distilling Company cast a long shadow over Commercial Street in Boston on January 15, 1919. Fifty-eight feet high and ninety feet across, its great curved steel sides glistened in the sun. On this Wednesday afternoon the massive tank held 2.5 million gallons of molasses. The sun that warmed the city also warmed the molasses in the tank. The thick syrup bubbled and grew, pushing against the sides of the tank! Then a low rumble came from the tank.

Freight horses stamped and neighed as the ground trembled under their feet. The rumble became a dull, muffled roar. Without warning the top of the tank exploded. Two and a half million gallons of molasses poured down on Commercial Street, overturning wagons. The flood turned into a smelly river of vegetables, machine parts, and wagon wheels. The wave picked up one fireman and tossed him into the harbor. Like a high diver he landed in the water and was picked up by a fireboat. The wall of molasses rolled along, picking up everything in its path. Firemen stretched ladders over the thick goo to reach trapped people. By the time the molasses flood trickled to a stream, 21 people had lost their lives and 150 people were injured. When the molasses flood finally ceased, cleaning up the sticky mess was nearly impossible. In fact, some people say the smell of molasses still lingers on a hot summer day on Commercial Street.

**Describe** the Great Molasses Disaster using this pattern. **Standards** I-B, C, D, E

The sticky molasses poured

From _____

Through _____

Across _____

Around _____

Between _____

Beneath _____

Near _____

Into _____

# RESEARCH REPORT: DISASTERS

**Read about** one of these historical disasters. Summarize the disaster using the preposition poetry model below. **Standards** I-B, C, D, E; III-E, F, G

1811–1812 New Madrid earthquake

1906 San Francisco Earthquake

1912 Sinking of the *Titanic*

1918 Flu epidemic

1937 Burning of the *Hindenburg*

1986 Explosion of the space shuttle *Challenger*

1986 Nuclear disaster: Chernobyl (Russia)

1989 San Francisco Earthquake

1989 *Exxon-Valdez* oil spill

1993 Midwest floods

2001 Two Boeing 767s hit World Trade Center and Pentagon

2006 Hurricane Katrina

The _____

From _____

Through _____

Across _____

Around _____

Between _____

Beneath _____

Near _____

Into _____

# QUIZ: WORLD WAR II: OPERATION MINCEMEAT (1940–1945)

Operation Mincemeat was a secret plan by the British to fool the German High Command into thinking the British would invade Sardinia rather than Sicily in World War II.

The family of a young man recently deceased agreed to allow the British to take their son's body and send it out to sea, where it would be found by the Germans. The family agreed to the plan on the condition that their son's name would never be revealed. The British named the body Major William Martin. On the body were highly secret papers telling of the British invasion of Sardinia, along with letters from a fake girlfriend, keys, theater stubs, and an overdue bill from his club.

A local fisherman found the body and reported the discovery to the Germans. Because the young man died of pneumonia, his lungs were filled with fluid, which led the Germans to believe he had drowned. They carefully removed the papers and photographed them, then gave them to Spanish officials, who returned the papers to the British.

German intelligence believed that the British would attack Sardinia and were unprepared when the attack on Sicily took place. Major William Martin, though not alive, saved many British lives.

**Research:** Every country has a spy agency to gather information about other countries. Match each intelligence-gathering agency with its country. **Standards** III-C, D, E

| | | |
|---|---|---|
| 1. _____ United States | | a. SAVAK |
| 2. _____ Great Britain | | b. BND |
| 3. _____ Russia | | c. MOSSAD |
| 4. _____ France | | d. CIA |
| 5. _____ Israel | | e. BOSS |
| 6. _____ Germany | | f. SIS |
| 7. _____ South Africa | | g. KGB |
| 8. _____ Iran | | h. DTS |

**Answer Key:** 1-d; 2-f; 3-g; 4-h; 5-c; 6-b; 7-e; 8-a

# THE DANCER WAS A SPY (1939–1945)

No one was smiling in 1939 when the flags of Nazi Germany went up in Poland. Soon the world was at war. Less than a year later Germany invaded France. High-ranking officers took over stately homes, where they gave receptions and parties. They asked Josephine Baker, a famous stage star, to perform at their parties. Josephine was an American living in France.

"But of course you will not dance for them," her French friends advised.

"But I must," Josephine replied, and she did. Josephine flitted from one embassy to another. The Germans thought her a fine entertainer and invited her to many parties. French citizens called her a traitor for entertaining the enemy. Some spit at her if they saw her on the street.

Only the leaders of the Free French knew why Josephine danced for the Germans. At the end of each dance she would chat with high-ranking officers. The Germans talked freely. She learned about troop movements and locations. She obtained an important code book.

Week after week Josephine gathered information. Her difficult task was to get the information to the Free French in unoccupied France. If she were caught carrying enemy secrets, she would be shot. She passed the information to the Free French in invisible ink on her sheet music. More enemy secrets were pinned to her underwear.

For four years Josephine's stage was a world at war. For four years she pretended to be a traitor. For four years she lived with the scorn of the French people. It was a most difficult and dangerous part to play. At the end of the war, when her secret could be told, a grateful France awarded Josephine its highest military honors.

# RESEARCH REPORT: RESEARCHING WOMEN SPIES (1776–1865)

For four years during World War II, Josephine Baker passed along enemy secrets to the Free French as she traveled throughout France and into Spain, accompanied by her favorite pet. In her suitcase she might have had:

Dancing costumes: for her performances

Diamond jewelry: to dazzle the border guards

Cheetah food: so her pet would not go hungry

Invisible ink: to write code messages on her sheet music

Safety pins: to pin important information gained from the enemy to her underclothes.

Everyday clothing: for those times she was not on stage

A party dress: for attending parties given by the Germans

**Read about** one of the following famous women spies from American history. List six to eight items the spy might have carried with her on her travels. Tell why she would need each item. **Standards** I-A, B, E; II-A, C, D, I; III-D, F

| | | |
|---|---|---|
| Sybil Ludington | Nancy Hart | Mary Elizabeth Bowser |
| Mary Touvestre | Emily Geiger | Ginny Moon |
| Emeline Piggott | Antonia Ford | Lottie Moon |
| Elizabeth Van Lew | Pauline Cushman | Rose Greenhow |

Name _____     Spy During _____

Item                                                Why?

_____     _____

_____     _____

_____     _____

_____     _____

_____     _____

_____     _____

_____     _____

_____     _____

# RESEARCH REPORT:
# THE BING CROSBY CODE (1975)

During the Vietnam War, the code for American troops to withdraw upon the fall of Saigon in April 1975 was when they heard Bing Crosby sing "White Christmas" on the radio.

## THE VIETNAM VETERANS MEMORIAL

The Vietnam Veterans Memorial honors the men and women of the armed forces of the United States who served in the Vietnam War. On it are listed the names of those who gave their lives and those missing in action. The memorial is located in Washington, D.C. A major theme of the memorial is that of making people aware of the impact of war and to understand the price that has to be paid in human lives.

**Find out the following. Standards** III-C, D, E, G, H

1. Who designed the Wall? _____

2. When was it dedicated? _____

3. How long is the Wall? _____

4. How many names are written on the Wall? _____

**Answer Key:** 1-Maya Yang Lin; 2-11/18/82; 3-493 ft.; 4-58,000

## RESPONDING WITH POETRY

Use the following poetry model to describe the Vietnam Veterans Memorial. Follow the directions for each line.

1. one word: subject noun _____

2. two words: adjectives _____

3. three words: participles _____

4. four words: nouns related to the subject _____

_____

5. three words: participles _____

6. two words: adjectives _____

7. one word: noun, opposite of the subject _____

# RESEARCH REPORT:
# YESTERDAY AND TODAY (1900-200_)

Here are facts from the 1900s. **Compare** each item with your life today. **Standards** I-A, D, F, I; II-I; III-D, E, F, G

In 1900 the average teacher's pay was $325 a year.

Today the average teacher's salary in your town is _____

In 1906 the automobile speed limit in most states was 20 miles per hour.

Today the highway speed limit in your state is _____ miles per hour.

In 1900 the first Eastman Kodak Brownie Camera cost $1.00.

Today the average price of a digital camera is _____

In 1905 life expectancy for men was 48 years.

Today life expectancy for men is _____ years.

In 1930 a loaf of bread cost eight cents.

Today a loaf of bread costs _____.

In 1930 no American home had a television.

Today _____ percent of American homes have one or more televisions.

In 1942 Americans were allowed to buy two gallons of gas a week and two pairs of leather shoes a year.

Today _____

_____

# RESEARCH REPORT:
# A HISTORICAL BIRTHDAY CARD

**Research** the items in boldface type for the year a friend or family member was born. **Design** a birthday card with the following information. **Standards** I-B, C, D; II-A, G; III-D, G, H

**Example:** 1945, THE YEAR YOU WERE BORN!

1.  **President:** Franklin Delano Roosevelt; Vice president, Harry Truman

2.  **Secretary of War:** Robert P. Patterson

3.  **English Monarch:** George VI

4.  **Pope:** Pius XII

5.  **Nobel Prize for Medicine:** Sir Alexander Fleming (penicillin)

6.  **Nobel Prize for Literature:** Jon Hersey

7.  **Academy Award for Best Actor:** Ray Milland

8.  **Academy Award for Best Actress:** Joan Crawford

9.  **Miss America:** Bess Myerson

10. **Three popular songs:**

    a.  "On the Atchison, Topeka and Santa Fe"

    b.  "There, I've Said I Again"

    c.  "Sentimental Journey"

11. **Kentucky Derby Winner:** Hoop Jr.

12. **World Series Winner:** Detroit

| | |
|---|---|
| **1945**<br><br>**Here are Presidents, Songs, and Prizes, too** | **But the most important thing that happened was**<br><br>**YOU!**<br><br>**Happy Birthday!** |

# Resources: History

## CIVIL WAR

*Billy Yank and Johnny Reb,* by Susan Beller. 21st Century Books, 2000.
    Describes the lives of soldiers on both sides of the conflict.

*Bull Run,* by Paul Fleischman. HarperCollins, 1993.
    Fictional characters tell about their Civil War experiences.

*The Civil War,* by Anne Devereaux Jordan. Benchmark Books, 2007.
    Features the participation of African Americans.

*Civil War from A-Z,* by Norm Bolotin. Dutton, 2002.
    A guide to people, places, and points of interest.

*Daring Women of the Civil War,* by Carin T. Ford. Enslow Publishers, 2004.
    Includes those who served as spies.

## ALAMO

*The Alamo,* by Dennis B. Fradin. Benchmark Books, 2007.
    The battle as well as the events that preceded and followed it.

*Susannah of the Alamo,* by John Jakes. HarperCollins, 1995.
    The story of the siege of the Alamo and the brave woman who, with her child, was among the few who survived.

## WILD WEST

*Buffalo Gals: Women of the Wild West,* by Brandon Miller. Lerner Publications, 1995.
    The hard work and the exciting challenges faced by women who settled the West.

*Children of the Wild West,* by Russell Feedman. Clarion, 1983.
    Growing up in the Old West.

*Cockeyed Charlie Parkhurst,* by Craig McDonald. Filter Press, 1973.
    Story of the West's most unusual stage whip.

*Ghost Towns of the American West,* by Raymond Bial. Houghton Miffllin, 2001.
    Photographs and information on ghost towns.

*Lost Dutchman Mine,* by Robert Sikorsky. Golden West Publishing, 1991
    Quest for the Dutchman's gold, a 100-year-old mystery.

*Remember Little Bighorn,* by Paul Robert Walker. National Geographic, 2006.
    Indians and soldiers recount Custer's last stand.

## WOMEN'S SUFFRAGE

*Created Equal,* by Ann Rossi. National Geographic, 2005.

Women campaign for the right to vote.

*Ladies First,* by Elizabeth Kimmel. National Geographic, 2006.

Stories of 40 daring American women.

*33 Things Every Girl Should Know About Women's History.* Edited by Tonya Bolden. Crown, 2002.

Women's history from colonial days to the 20th century.

## DISASTERS

*Earthquakes: Disaster and Survival,* by Jennifer Reed. Enslow, 2004.

Stories of survivors of and rescuers in major earthquakes.

*Flood,* by Patricia Lauber. National Geographic 1996.

Vivid descriptions of the 1927 and 1993 flooding of the Mississippi River and the effect on the people of the Midwest.

*The Great Fire,* by Jim Murphy. Scholastic, 1995.

An account of the 1871 Chicago fire, with firsthand descriptions.

*Hurricanes, Tsunamis and Natural Disasters,* by Andrew Langley. Kingfisher, 2006.

Causes and effects of a variety of natural disasters.

## SPIES

*Spies,* by Clive Gifford. Kingfisher, 2004.

History of spies, with stories of actual spies.

## WORLD WAR II

*The Good Fight,* by Stephen Ambrose. Atheneum, 2001.

How World War II was won.

*Remember D Day,* by Ronald Drez. National Geographic, 2004.

The plan, the invasion, and survivor stories.

*Remember World War II,* by Dorinda Nicholson. National Geographic, 2005.

Kids who survived tell their stories.

*World War II,* by Simon Adams. DK Publishers, 2004.

Major events of the war with photographs.

# Part Nine

# The Earth and Its Creatures

## Amazing Earth Facts

The North Pole has no land, only ice above water.

New Zealand has the largest boiling lake in the world.

Forest fires move faster uphill than downhill.

The sun is 330,330 times larger than the earth.

In some places on the earth it has rained fish and snakes.

An earthquake caused the Mississippi River to run backward.

In Scotland the desert sands sing.

## Amazing Creature Facts

Elephants spend 23 hours a day eating.

Snakes can see through their eyelids.

The kea bird of New Zealand likes to eat rubber strips around car windows.

A mole can dig 300 feet in one night.

A cockroach can live weeks with its head cut off.

Over 10,000 birds die a year from smashing into windows.

There are more than one million animal species on the earth.

Hummingbirds weigh less than a penny.

# RESEARCH REPORT:
# WHEN THE RIVER RAN BACKWARDS

December 16, 1811, saw a quiet dawn in the sleepy frontier town of New Madrid, Missouri. It was a tiny town with few settlers, which turned out to be very good thing. At first the sleeping settlers felt nothing, then the hanging kerosene lamps began to swing. Pots and pans rattled, and folks ran outdoors, feeling a trembling of the ground under their feet. Before long home-made furniture in the cabins moved and overturned. Folks outdoors found it hard to stand up. Stone chimneys fell, and less sturdy cabins collapsed. There was general panic as more and more buildings fell. Those folks not injured or killed watched in astonishment as the mighty Mississippi River ran backwards, flooding the land and creating a large lake. Two more huge quakes followed, on January 23 and February 7, 1812, destroying forests and tearing up land for over 5,000 square miles. Aftershocks of the 8.0 (Richter Scale, 10.5 Mercalli scale) quakes were felt for a full year.

**Research** the Mercalli Scale. Create a cartoon sketch of one thing that might happen at each level of the scale, 5.0 to 10.0. **Standards** I-B, C, D; II-A, G; III-D, G, H

| 5.0 | 6.0 | 7.0 |
|-----|-----|-----|
| 8.0 | 9.0 | 10.0 |

**Answer Key:** Possible drawings: 5.0 doors open, small objects drop; 6.0 furniture overturned; 7.0 hard to stand, chimneys fall; 8.0 partial collapse of buildings; 9.0 panic, complete collapse of buildings; 10.0 total destruction, river runs backward

# MNEMONICS

## THE SEVEN CONTINENTS: A MOSTLY TRUE STORY

In 1889 Nellie Bly, a reporter for the *New York Times*, read a book by Jules Verne, *Around the World in Eighty Days*. "I can beat that record," she said, and she set sail from New York Harbor to do just that. Her first stops were in Europe, where she visited Jules Verne in France. She moved on to Italy, and from there she set sail for Africa. She continued her journey on Egyptian camels, then traveled by boat up the Suez Canal. It's a fact that Nellie moved through Africa faster than a flea can sneeze.

"Amazing," people said. "She is tireless. How can a mere woman move so fast from one time zone to another and not collapse from exhaustion?" Nellie had a secret that she never told anyone. Because of her secret, she paid no attention to those who thought women were the weaker sex. She left Africa, and made stops in six different Asian countries. She stepped over a cobra in Sri Lanka, clung to a ship's mast in a monsoon off Hong Kong, and celebrated Christmas in China. Having no fondness for penguins or kangaroos, she skipped Antarctica and Australia but adopted a monkey in Singapore. Setting sail from Yokohama, she bypassed South America on her way to San Francisco. Nellie moved like a whirlwind. Nellie beat the record! Since she never stopped to rest even though she experienced many sleepless nights, she made her trip around the world in 72 days!

Nellie never told anyone the secret of how she maintained such a high energy level. It is revealed here for the first time. To be a world traveler who never tires:

| **E**-at | **A**-n | **A**-pple | **A**-fter | **A** | **S**-leepless | **N**-ight |
|----------|---------|------------|------------|-------|----------------|------------|
| Europe | Africa | Asia | Antarctica | Australia | South America | North America |

# MNEMONICS: THE BOILING LAKE

Imagine living on a lush green island with a large lake in its center but not being able to go fishing or swimming in the lake. This is the volcanic island of Dominica, and its lake boils like a witch's cauldron, giving off acrid steaming fumes of sulfur. Before reaching the lake a traveler would pass through lush green valleys and sparkling rivers that slide over wondrous waterfalls. But the beauty ends at the Valley of Desolation, where nothing grows except slimy mosses and brown scree. The waters of the streams flow inky black or milky yellow. A difficult climb takes you to the edge of a volcanic crater, where down below the waters of the lake churn, bubble, and steam with poisonous fumes that can kill. Only one other boiling lake in the world is larger; it is found in New Zealand.

## A WORLD OF MNEMONICS!

"New mon icks." What a strange word! It comes from the name of the Greek goddess of memory and means mindful. Sometimes our MINDS are so FULL of new information that it is hard to remember it all.

SO: To remember notes on a scale, music students recite "Every Good Boy Does Fine": E, G, B, D, F

Anything is easier to remember if you connect it with a story. Read the story on the previous page to help you remember the seven continents.

**Create a story** to help others remember the five Great Lakes. **Standards** II-A, B, D, I, K, L

**H**-uron     **O**-ntario     **M**-ichigan     **E**-rie     **S**-uperior

_____

_____

_____

_____

_____

_____

_____

_____

_____

_____

_____

_____

# TREASURE ISLAND

Cocos Island, a small island 300 miles south of Costa Rica, has had its share of visitors. These visitors are not tourists, because the island has only one small harbor, a steep coastline of 600-foot cliffs, no sandy beaches, and no fancy hotel. The island is hot and humid, and it rains nearly every day between March and December, so most of the island is dense jungle.

Why, then, have more than 300 expeditions made their way to the island? Not to view the cocoanut palms, from which it gets its name. They come to find the treasure!

Some say the island holds the richest treasure in the world just waiting to be found. The first treasure was buried by a pirate who raided cities along the Pacific Coast.

The second treasure arrived in 1821. In order to hide the wealth of Lima from invaders, the governor of Lima and the heads of the church asked Captain Thompson to take the treasures aboard his ship, the *Mary Dear*, to keep it safe. Spanish guards were sent along to protect the treasure, but the guards were no match for a greedy crew. The sailors killed the guards and took the ship to Cocos Island, where they hid tons of precious gold and gems.

Many expeditions have arrived over the years hoping to find the treasure. In 1897 300 British sailors arrived and scoured the 5-mile-by-21.5-mile island. They went home empty handed. From time to time a few gold coins have been found, but never in the same place. To this day the island refuses to give up its treasure.

# RESEARCH REPORT: RESEARCHING PIRATES

Most pirates are remembered for their dastardly deeds and have few, if any, redeeming qualities. Among the most infamous are Edward Teach, William Kidd, and Mary Bonney.

One pirate, however, was pardoned by the U.S. government for the help he gave Andrew Jackson during the War of 1812. His name was Jean Laffite.

**Find out more** about Jean Laffite and use the pattern below to write about him. **Standards** I-B, C, D, E; II-A, D, G; III-B, C, D, E ,F

**The Pattern**

| | |
|---|---|
| NAME | NAME |
| My name is Edward Teach | My name is _____ |
| I AM (5 ATTRIBUTES) | I AM |
| A former privateer for the British | _____ |
| Master of a 40-gun warship | _____ |
| Notorious for outrages along the Eastern Coast | _____ |
| | _____ |
| Toll collector for shipping in the Pamlico Sound | _____ |
| Keeper of the secret of my vast buried treasure | _____ |
| I WONDER | I WONDER |
| When the governor of North Carolina will reject our prize-sharing agreement? | _____ |
| | _____ |
| | _____ |
| MY LEGACY IS | MY LEGACY IS |
| My luxuriant, thick facial hair, from which I got my nickname, BLACKBEARD! | _____ |
| | _____ |
| | _____ |

# CREATIVE WRITING: STRANGE RAINS

- The July 12, 1873 issue of *Scientific American* reported that a shower of frogs fell over Kansas City, Missouri, during a rainstorm.

- The same magazine reported in May 1877 that a shower of snakes fell on Memphis, Tennessee.

- The September 1949 issue of *Nature Magazine* contained an article by A. D. Bajkov reporting a shower of fish over Marksville, Louisiana.

**Creative writing:** Suppose you were a citizen of one of the cities above and experienced the strange rain. Follow the outline below to tell what might happen and how you would react. **Standards** I-B, C, F; II-A, D

It was a warm day in (month) _____ of (year) _____ when the rain began I was (where?) _____ (doing what?) _____, when I realized I was seeing more than raindrops. Along with the heavy rain came dozens of _____ _____.

I was so startled that I _____. I wasn't the only one who was amazed at seeing the _____. (Name a person) _____ took one look and _____ (Name a second person) _____ was as amazed as I was. He/she _____. When the rain ended we had to find a way to get rid of the _____, so we _____ and _____, and that was the end of that.

You probably think this is a tall tale but it really did rain _____ _____. No kidding!

# CREATIVE WRITING: SINGING SANDS

Off the west coast of Scotland lies the remote Isle of Eigg. It is a desolate place with jagged mountains and immense stretches of white sand. However, the Isle has many visitors. Why? To hear the sands sing. A footstep will start the music. If the sands are run slowly through the fingers, the notes that are heard range from very high to very low. Nowhere else on Earth have singing sands been found.

Scientists believe they have solved the mystery of the singing sands. When put under a microscope the grains appear to be perfectly round. When analyzed for content they are made of fine ground mineral quartz. Any movement causes the sands to rub together to produce the musical notes.

**Pretend** you have taken a walk through the Singing Sands. Complete the lines below. **Standards** I-B, C, F; II-A, D

I remember the smell _____

_____

And the feel _____

_____

And the magical hour spent _____

_____

And the sounds of _____

_____

And the joyous feeling of _____

_____

As I _____

_____

That is why the Singing Sands _____

_____

# ENDANGERED SPECIES

## DID YOU KNOW . . .

- Unless we work to protect animals on the earth, 25 percent of all species that now exist will be gone within 20 years. See *Going Green,* by John Elkington.

- Animals now living on the earth are disappearing 10,000 times faster than they did before humans arrived on the earth. See *Protecting Endangered Species,* by Felicity Brooks.

- 98 percent of the 500 million species that have existed on the earth since the beginning of time are extinct. See *Ripley's Believe It Or Not: Wild Animals.*

- A dolphin lives an average of 6 years in captivity but 25 years in the wild. Source: U.S. Fish and Wildlife Services.

- 45 percent of Hawaii's native birds no longer exist. Source: Hawaii Conservation Commission.

## AN INFINITIVE POEM PATTERN

### The Grizzly Bear

All I wanted was
to roam freely from Mexico to Alaska
to grow unhindered to my full eight feet and 900 pounds
to find ample game, fish and berries to satisfy my hunger
to see my silver-tipped brown fur sparkle in the sunlight
to find a cozy den in which to curl up in the winter
to be protected in National Parks

But I didn't want
to face big game hunters who kill for sport
to have my head stuffed and placed on a wall
to find my food supply gone as cities spread out
to be confined to s single area, a tiny part of the land I once roamed
to have my beautiful fur made into a rug
to become one of many endangered species

# RESEARCH REPORT: ENDANGERED SPECIES

**Fact:** There are more than 1,200 endangered species of plants and animals in the United States. Source: U.S. Fish and Wildlife Service

**Research** the life and habits of an endangered animal. Use this infinitive poem pattern to **report your information. Standards** I-B, C, D, E; II-A, D, G; III-B, C, D, E, F

### All I wanted was . . .

to _____

to _____

to _____

to _____

to _____

to _____

### But I didn't want . . .

to _____

to _____

to _____

to _____

to _____

to _____

# MARVELOUS MAMMALS

## FAINTING GOATS

Back in the 1880s there was a fellow named Tinsley who never stayed in one place very long. He moved from one small farm or village to another, accompanied by a small herd of goats. Tinsley never had to worry about being attacked by wild critters. When the goats sensed a wild creature coming near they would faint, falling on their backs with their legs up in the air. It wasn't a pretend faint but a real one. Sometimes the wild creature went on its way, then the goats would recover from their faint and hop to their feet.

It seems that Tinsley was short of money and met a farmer whose sheep were being attacked by wild dogs or coyotes. He sold his fainting goats to the farmer. When the sheep were attacked, the fainting goats caught the attention of the coyotes, and the sheep were able to run away. As you can imagine, fainting goats are very rare today.

Another animal that faints when it senses danger is the opossum. Its body becomes rigid and can be poked, prodded, or rolled over with no reaction. Since many predators won't eat game they have not killed, the opossum stays motionless until the predator has moved on to other prey.

## SUICIDAL LEMMINGS

The Lapland lemmings live in the mountains and multiply rapidly. When the food supply runs short, the lemmings begin a march in a straight line, stripping the earth of any vegetation in their way. Nothing stops them. They will walk between a man's legs, gnaw through a haystack, and swim across a lake until they come to the sea, where they swim out as far as they can and then drown. A few survive and make their way back to the mountains to start another herd.

# CREATIVE WRITING: MORE MARVELOUS MAMMALS

## SPEEDERS

A kangaroo can't walk, but it can hop at 40 miles per hour.

A greyhound can run at 40 miles per hour.

A racehorse can run at 45 to 50 miles per hour.

An antelope can run at 60 miles per hour.

A cheetah can run at 70 miles per hour; it is the fastest of all mammals.

## SMALL BUT MIGHTY

Woe to the lion that attacks a porcupine. Although the porcupine does not shoot its quills, they do come off easily. A lion foolish enough to attach a porcupine will end up with a mouth full of quills. The tip of each quill is like a fish hook. The more the lion tries to get rid of the quills, the more deeply embedded they become. Within a few days the lion is unable to eat and dies of starvation.

The smallest mammal in the world is the shrew. It is two inches long and weighs less than a quarter. However, the shrew is one of the most dangerous of all mammals. It has a poisonous bite like a cobra, eats twice its weight every day, and will attack an animal three times its size.

Rudyard Kipling wrote his *Just So Stories* to explain certain animal characteristics, such as how the elephant got its trunk or how the leopard got its spots.

**Choose** one of these animals. **Create a story** that tells:

Why Goats Faint When Frightened

Why Opossum Plays Dead

Why Lemmings March to the Sea

Why Kangaroo Can't Walk

Why Cheetah Is the Fastest Runner

How the Porcupine Got Its Quills

Why Shrew Eats Twice Its Weight

Your story must have a beginning to introduce the animal, a middle in which the animal has a problem, and an end, where the problem is solved. Use the worksheet on page 142 to develop your story. **Standards** I-B, C, F; II-A, D

# CREATIVE WRITING: STORY OUTLINE

**Story Statement**

This is a story about _____

who wanted _____

but couldn't because _____

until _____

**Introduction** (Introduce the animal and its setting)

_____

_____

_____

**The Problem:** What problem does the animal have?

_____

_____

_____

**The Solution:** Explain how a particular characteristic (e.g., goats fainting, lemmings marching, kangaroos hopping, cheetahs running, porcupines with quills. shrews eating) is part of the solution to the problem.

_____

_____

_____

_____

_____

_____

_____

_____

# CREATIVE WRITING:
# THE _____
# ENJOYS A HOLIDAY!

### THE CAIMAN: LIFE AFTER DEATH

Smaller than an alligator, the caiman can bite a man's arm off at least a half hour after it is dead. It lives in the jungles of Brazil. Dr. Fred Medem, professor of zoology at the University of Bogota, has been bitten twice by a caiman after its neck was broken.

### THE PYTHON: A YEAR-LONG DIET

Because they go long periods of time barely moving, pythons can go a full year without food. Boa constrictors have the same ability. Because snakes are cold-blooded, they don't need food to keep their bodies warm.

### THE BLUE WHALE: THE LARGEST ANIMAL

Measuring 120 feet long and weighing and up to 120 tons, the blue whale is larger than any dinosaur that ever roamed the earth. It is longer than a city block but only eats tiny, shrimplike creatures. It is a mammal, yet can stay under water 30 minutes.

### THE CROCODILE'S TOOTHBRUSH: THE PLOVER

The plover is a small bird that fearlessly hops between the crocodile's open jaws and cleans morsels from the crocodile's teeth. The crocodile never closes its jaws on the plover, waiting until its teeth are clean and the small bird has flown away.

Send one of these creatures on a holiday. **Complete the information below. Standards** I-B, C, F; II-A, D

Animal _____

Holiday _____

Description and action verbs related to the animal _____

Where will the animal spend the holiday? _____

How will it get there? _____

What will it take along? _____

What will happen? _____

# ANIMAL HEROES

## BINTI JUA

In July 2006 a three-year-old little boy climbed over a railing at the zoo and fell 18 feet into the gorilla exhibit. A female gorilla, Binti Jua, with her baby, Koala, on her back, picked up the injured child and gently carried him to a spot where humans took over. After four days in the hospital the child went home to his family.

## BUCKY

In May 2007 a 72-year-old man had just caught a bass and was releasing it when Bucky, his dog, tipped the boat over. The man knew it was too far to swim to shore, so he clung to the overturned boat. Bucky, however, swam to shore and raised the alarm. The fisherman was rescued after about four minutes in the water.

## TYSON

In December 2006 a British youth was set upon by thugs and beaten unconscious. The youth's dog, Tyson, kept him warm by stretching out next to him until help came. Doctors said that because of the bitter winter temperatures, the boy would have died without the dog to keep him warm.

## ALFIE

In July 2006 in Philadelphia a two-year-old climbed out a second story window and began a journey that took him across eight rooftops. Alfie, the family's German shepherd, followed the child from one rooftop to the next while barking to attract attention. Neighbors rescued the child.

## SELVAKUMAR

The terrible tsunami in December 2004 claimed many lives. One small boy, however, is alive today because of the family pet. As the massive waves rolled over the village, the child was picked up and carried along on the crest of a wave. The family dog, Selvakumar, grabbed the child by his shirt and hung on to him until the wave passed. The child's mother, who thought he was lost, was overjoyed to find him in the clutches of Selvakumar.

# RESEARCH REPORT: THE NEWSHOUND!

**Create** an animal newspaper. **Research** strange or unusual animals and/or animal heroes. All facts must be accurate. **Standards** I-B, C, D, E, F; II-C, D, F

| | |
|---|---|
| **Headline News: DATE** _____ <br> _____ **SAVES** _____ <br> _____ <br> _____ <br> _____ <br> _____ <br> _____ <br> _____ <br> _____ <br> _____ <br> _____ <br> _____ <br> _____ | **EDITORIAL** <br> **Research dog racing. Write an editorial for or against it.** <br> _____ <br> _____ <br> _____ <br> _____ <br> _____ <br> _____ <br> _____ <br> _____ <br> _____ <br> _____ |
| **ADVERTISEMENT** <br> **Visit a pet supply store. Write ads for the most expensive items you can buy for a pet.** <br> _____ <br> _____ <br> _____ <br> _____ <br> _____ <br> _____ <br> _____ <br> _____ <br> _____ <br> _____ | **BOOK REVIEW** <br> **Write a brief review of a new book that features an animal.** <br> **Title** _____ <br> **Author** _____ <br> _____ <br> _____ <br> _____ <br> _____ <br> _____ <br> _____ <br> _____ <br> _____ |

# Resources:
# The Earth and Its Creatures

*Almost Gone,* by Ron Hirshi. HarperCollins, 2006.

   A look at the world's rarest animals.

*Animals in Motion,* by Pamela Hickman. Kids Can Press, 2000.

   How animals swim, jump, slither, and glide.

*Biggest, Strongest, Fastest,* by Steve Jenkins. Ticknor & Fields, 1995.

   Information on record-setting animals.

*Claws, Coats & Camouflage,* by Susan Goodman. Millbrook, 2001.

   The ways animals fit into their world.

*Earthquakes,* by Franklyn Branley. HarperCollins, 2005.

   Causes and effects of earthquakes.

*Forces of Nature,* by Catherine Grace. National Geographic, 2004.

   The power of volcanoes, earthquakes, and tornadoes

*Hurricane Hunters: Riders on the Storm,* by Chris Demarest. Atheneum, 2006.

   Planes that collect hurricane date by flying into the storms.

*In the Wild,* by Sneed B Collard III. Benchmark, 2006.

   Efforts by zoologists to save endangered animals.

*Planet Earth: Inside Out,* by Gail Gibbons. Morrow Junior Books, 19915.

   Brief explanations of the earth's interior.

*Searching for Grizzlies,* by Ron Hirschi. Boyds Mill, 2005.

   Characteristics and behavior of grizzly bears.

*Snakes! Strange and Wonderful,* by Laurence Pringle. Boyds Mills Press 2004.

   Characteristics and behavior of three dozen snakes.

*The Truth About Dangerous Sea Creatures,* by Mary Cerullo. Chronicle, 2003.

   Excellent information on a variety of dangerous sea animals.

*Tsunamis,* by Thomas Adamson. Capstone Press, 2005.

   Causes, effects, and movements of tsunamis

*What Do You Do When Something Wants to Eat You?,* by Steve Jenkins. Houghton Mifflin, 1997.

   How various animals escape from predators.

*Wild Science,* by Victoria Miles. Raincoast Books, 2004.

   Amazing encounters between animals and the people who study them.

# Part Ten

# The Unexplained

## Legend or Truth?

A "Fee Jee" mermaid is on display at the Peabody Museum of Harvard University.

In 1835 visitors flocked to see Joice Heth, the 161-year-old former nurse of George Washington.

In 1869 the fossil of a man, 10.5 feet tall, was unearthed on a New York farm.

More than 50 ships and 20 planes have mysteriously disappeared while traveling through the Bermuda Triangle.

Any owner of the Hope Diamond must be aware of its curse: bad luck or early death will follow ownership.

An abominable snowman makes its home in the massive Himalaya mountains, often seen but never captured.

In 1880 farmer David Lang disappeared in front of five witnesses. Later the grass where he stood turned yellow and formed a circle.

During World War II the German naval command called upon a priest to exorcise a ghost from one of its submarines.

# THE DEVIL SHIP

In 1916 the U-65 was one of 24 submarines built by the German naval command. Twenty-three of the submarines saw combat duty and were retired at the end of World War I. The U-65 was different. During construction a steel girder fell from a tightly secured sling, killing two workers. Nothing defective was found in the sling and such an accident was considered to be impossible, yet it happened.

In dry dock, the engine room door would not open. It had to be cut open, and three men were found dead inside from inhaling deadly gasses. On its first practice cruise the ship was taken deep beneath the surface of the water as expected, but despite the efforts of the crew, it would not rise again. The oxygen supply was nearly gone after 12 hours submerged. Crew members thought they were doomed when suddenly, on its own, the ship rose. Again the ship went to dry dock. Nothing was found to be wrong.

The ship was ordered to sea. When torpedoes were being loaded, one slipped and fell, killing an officer and four men. When the ship finally put to sea with a crew of 31, all was normal for the next 18 months. Then the captain and crew saw the officer who had been killed by the torpedo walking the decks. A priest was called upon to exorcise the ghost from the ship. A new captain and crew were assigned to the ship. The new captain was a "no-nonsense" man who did not believe in ghosts.

On the next trip out two sailors disappeared, and the chief engineer broke his leg. On July 31, 1918, the ship was declared missing and assumed lost at sea. Not long after. an American submarine off the Irish coast saw the U-65 moving along on the surface. As the American sailors watched, the U-65 blew up. There were no mines or other submarines in the area, and the American submarine had not fired a torpedo. It seemed the "Devil Ship" had destroyed itself.

# RESEARCH ACTIVITY: BALLAD OF HUNLEY'S BOATS

Many historic events are retold in ballads. Three ships designed by H. L. Hunley turned out to be "bad luck" ships during the Civil War.

**Read** about the Hunley disasters in the encyclopedia or on the Internet. **Add the missing words** to the ballad. **Standards** I-B, C, F; II-A, D

(First name) (1) _____ L. Hunley was a man with big ideas.
He believed in what the (2) (North/South) was fighting for.
So he took up pen and paper and he drew a fine design
For a (3) _____ to help to win the war.

Now his first craft built of wood measured (4) _____ feet long.
And it took (5) _____ men to turn the heavy crank.
But the first time that they tried to take the vessel out to sea.
It proved to be too heavy and it (6) _____.

Not one to give up easily, Hunley tried a second time
To build a ship to sail beneath the sea,
To attach a ticking bomb to an enemy ship's hull,
And quickly as it could attempt to flee.

There came a time of trial to see what the ship could do
And how long under water it could stay.
But before it met the enemy, before it could attack,
The Hunley ship went belly up in (7) _____ Bay.

But (first name) (8) _____ L. Hunley was a man with big ideas.
He believed in what the (9) (North/South) was fighting for.
So he built a third ship, built it better than the other two,
That would help the struggling (10) (North/South) to win the war.

With a 90-pound explosive on a line it drug behind,
And a brave and most determined eight man crew,
The Hunley ship attacked and blew to pieces a sturdy (11) (Northern/Southern) ship.
But sad to say the Hunley ship blew up, too.

**Answer Key:** 1-Horace; 2-South; 3-submarine; 4-34; 5-3; 6-sank; 7-Mobile; 8-Horace; 9-South; 10-South; 11-Northern

# THE P-40 GHOST PLANE

**Place the number** of each detail sentence in the box where it belongs. Then read about the P-40 ghost plane. **Standards** I-C, D, G

| A.  Radar reflections | B.  Fighters scrambled |
|---|---|
| C.  Evidence at crash site | D.  Possible explanations |

1. On December 8, 1942, radar picked up a plane heading for American soil.

2. He found parts of other planes and flew back toward his homeland.

3. They radioed that it was a bullet riddled P-40.

4. It did not appear to be an aerial attack.

5. The pilot was not found.

6. It flew from the direction of Japan in an overcast sky.

7. Two pilots were sent to intercept the plane.

8. Investigators were puzzled as to how the pilot could have taken off without landing gear.

9. The pilot, covered with blood, waved at them.

10. A diary indicated that the plane had come from 1,300 miles away.

11. The landing gear was missing

12. They watched while the plane smashed into the ground.

13.  American troops investigated the crash site.

14. There were no markings on the plane.

15. Perhaps the downed craft had been repaired by the pilot.

☠━☞ **Answer Key:** A-1, 4, 6; B-7, 3, 9, 11, 12; C-13, 5, 14, 10; D-15, 2, 8

# MYSTERIOUS PLACES: THE BERMUDA TRIANGLE

The Bermuda Triangle is that part of the Atlantic Ocean that forms a triangle, with its points being the southern coast of the United States, Bermuda, and the Greater Antilles. Since the mid-1800s more than 50 ships and 20 aircraft have mysteriously disappeared within the boundaries of the triangle. Some ships were found abandoned for no apparent reason. Other ships simply disappeared with no warning or distress signal given. Not a trace of a missing ship or aircraft has ever been found.

On the afternoon of December 5, 1945, five Avenger torpedo bombers left the Naval Air Station in Fort Lauderdale, Florida, for an overwater training flight. All of the pilots were highly qualified, with a senior qualified flight instructor in charge of the exercise. About two hours into the flight, the Naval Air Station picked up a message from the flight instructor to one of the other pilots. The message indicated that the exact location of the five planes was not clear. The compasses were not working, and excessive static from Cuban broadcasting stations made it impossible to contact the Florida Naval Air Station.

All radio contact was lost. The five planes on Flight 19 were never heard from again. An extensive search operation was launched, but no trace of the planes was ever found. A PBM patrol plane joined the search the evening of December 5 but was never seen or heard from after takeoff. It is believed the plane exploded, at sea but no trace of the plane or its crew was ever found.

There are many theories and speculations about the strange disappearances that have occurred over the Bermuda Triangle. Hundreds of ships and planes have journeyed into the area without incident.

# RESEARCH REPORT: MYSTERIOUS PLACES

EASTER ISLAND is an isolated island 2,300 miles off the west coast of Chile. The main village of Orongo sits between the volcano of Rano Kao and a sheer cliff drop-off. Rocks found at the village contain 150 carvings showing figures with a man's body and a bird's head. Today Easter Island is moving eastward toward South America by seafloor spreading, at the fastest rate known in the world.

THE LOST CITY OF ATLANTIS was supposedly located on an island-continent, west of the Mediterranean. It was described in detail by Plato. The city had peaceful, wealthy residents. It was a capital of trade, with abundant natural resources and a perfect climate. Legend says greed and corruption angered the gods so the city vanished in just one day. Experts believe a volcanic eruption caused the island to collapse and be sucked into the sea.

STONEHENGE is an earthwork, a bank and ditch with large stones 5,000 years old, located in Great Britain. It was possibly a worship or burial place. Legend says Merlin brought the stones from Ireland, where they were used for performing rituals and for healing. An awe-inspiring sight even though it's desolate and dilapidated.

**Choose** one of the places described above to read about. **List** 10 reasons why you would not want to visit there. Each reason should contain specific information about the place. **Standards** I-B, C, F; II-A, D

REASONS NOT TO VISIT _____

1. _____

2. _____

3. _____

4. _____

5. _____

6. _____

7. _____

8. _____

9. _____

10. _____

# ANCIENT CURSES

## THE MUMMY'S CURSE

In 1891 Howard, Carter, a young archaeologist, arrived in Egypt to search for the tomb of the young King Tutankhamen. His expedition was paid for the wealthy Lord Carnarvon. Thirty-one years later, in 1922, Carter found the hidden tomb and sent a telegram to Lord Carnarvon to come to Egypt for the opening. Twenty-two people were present when Carter made a hole in the door large enough to enter and discovered a wealth of treasures along with the gold coffin of the boy King Tut.

Rumor had it that Carter also discovered a stone tablet with the mummy's curse inscribed on it. Carter denied the rumor; however, a typical mummy's curse might have read: "As for any man who shall destroy these, it is the god Thoth who shall destroy him."

A few months after the opening of the tomb, Lord Carnarvon died from an infection on his face caused by an insect bite. When Tut's mummy was unwrapped, it had a wound on the left cheek in the same place as the insect bite suffered by Lord Carnarvon. By 1929 11 people who had had something to do with the discovery of the tomb had died early deaths of unnatural causes. The victims included Carter's personal secretary, Richard Bethell, and Bethell's father, Lord Westbury.

Modern science may have an explanation for the mummy's curse. Analysis of 40 mummies revealed the presence of mold spores, which can survive for thousands of years. When blown into the air and breathed, these mold spores can lead to organ failure and even death for people with weak immune systems. Today archaeologists wear protective gear to keep from breathing fungus or mold spores thousands of years old.

What do you think? Was the Mummy's Curse real or imagined?

## THE HOPE DIAMOND

Legend says that a curse of death would befall any who touched the large blue diamond stolen from an idol in India. It is known that the diamond was purchased in India in 1642 by Jean Taviernier, a French jeweler, who sold it to King Louis XIV. The gem eventually passed to Louis XVI, who with his queen, Marie Antionette, was beheaded. It was stolen during the French Revolution but reappeared in London in 1813. King George IV of England bought the diamond, but after his death it was sold to pay off debts. Subsequent owners of the diamond, it is said, have faced disaster or early death.

# WRITE AN OBITUARY

An *obituary* is found in a particular section of the newspaper. It is an official notice of a person's death, often accompanied by an account of his or her life and accomplishments.

**Check the local newspaper** for an example of an obituary. **Paste a sample here:**

Often a well-known person has a longer obituary, which gives more information about his or her life and accomplishments.

**Write** an obituary for King Tutankhamen. Include brief details of his life and at least two accomplishments. **Standards** I-B, C, D, E; II-A, D, G; III-B, C, D, E, F

---

---

---

---

---

---

# STRANGE CREATURES

## BIGFOOT

In 1974 a farmer in northern Montana reported that he went to investigate when his dogs were restless and emitting strange howls. The dogs refused to leave the shelter of the barn, although they seemed to be disturbed about something in the nearby woods. The farmer walked toward the woods, at the same time smelling a terrible odor. To the farmer's surprise, he saw a large hairy creature at the edge of the woods. It moved silently on two feet, from one tree to another. It was 12 to 15 feet tall, and as the farmer watched, it disappeared into the woods, uttering a high-pitched cry.

This account has been repeated many times by observers in the northwestern United States and western Canada. The first person to offer proof of such a creature's existence was David Thompson, an explorer, who in 1811 measured footprints of this unknown creature that were eight by twenty-four inches. In 1967 Californian Roger Patterson offered proof in the form of a somewhat fuzzy photograph.

Many feel that Bigfoot actually exists and is a cousin to the abominable snowman of the Himalayas, often called a yeti. Those who have seen the creature include a Polish soldier in 1942, who met two of the creatures a short distance away; Italian explorer A. N. Tombazi, who wrote of his encounter with the yeti in 1925; and two Norwegians, who in 1948 followed tracks that led them to a pair of yetis.

Does this humanlike creature actually exist? Most scientists think it does not. It seems strange that with all of the technology available today, no one has actually filmed or captured the creature. What do you think?

## THE LOCH NESS MONSTER

Nessie lives in a freshwater lake in Scotland. She is described as a plesiosaur, an extinct aquatic reptile. Many people have claimed to have seen, her moving along with her long neck extending from the water, One rather famous photograph shows a large, dark object gliding on the surface of the lake. Scientists, however, doubt Nessie's existence. The food supply in the lake, they say, is limited, and the plesiosaur is a sight hunter that could not find enough food in the peat-stained water. In addition, the plesiosaur is a cold-blooded reptile that requires warm tropical waters for life. The temperature in Loch Ness is 42 degrees Fahrenheit.

# RESEARCH ACTIVITY: THE RHYMING ACROSTIC

**Write** a rhyming acrostic about Bigfoot that includes factual information. Note the example given for Nessie, the Loch Ness monster. **Standards** I-B, C, F; II-A, D

**N** eck extending above peat-stained water

**E** xtinct plesiosaur, Neptune's daughter

**S** cientists dispute the creature's existence

**S** ay not enough food for Nessie's subsistence

**I** nsist that sightings are a joke or a hoax

**E** ven so Loch Ness attracts lots of folks


B  _____

I  _____

G  _____

F  _____

O  _____

O  _____

T  _____

# Resources:
# The Unexplained

*Extraordinary Events and Oddball Occurrences,* by Gary Blackwood. Benchmark Books, 1999
> Strange appearances, disappearances, and things falling from the sky.

*The Ghost Book,* by William Jasperjohn. Watts, 1989.
> Introduction to psychic elements, from ancient Greece to today.

*Ghost Liners,* by Robert Ballard. Little, Brown, 1998.
> Explanations of the world's greatest lost ships.

*Ghosts of the Deep,* by Daniel Cohen. Putnam, 1993.
> Encounters with ghosts aboard ship.

*The Headless Ghost,* by William E. Warren. Prentice-Hall, 1986.
> Ghosts, poltergeists, and tales of the unexplained

*How to Find a Ghost,* by James Deem. Houghton Mifflin, 1988.
> Instructions for becoming a ghost detective.

*Miracles: Opposing Viewpoints,* by Michael Arvey. Greenhaven Press, 1990.
> Saints, stigmata, miracle healings, and images explored.

*Mysterious Healing,* by Brian Innes. Raintree, 1999.
> Accounts of unexplained healing.

*Mysterious Places,* by Peter Hepplewhite. Sterling, 1997.
> From Stonehenge to Easter Island, a look at strange locales.

*The Restless Dead,* by Jim Razzi. Harper Trophy, 1994.
> Strange real-life mysteries.

*The Supernatural,* by Rhiannon Lassiter. Gareth Stevens, 2006.
> Explanation of parapsychology.

*Twenty-Five Scariest Places in the World,* by Phyllis Emert. Lowell House, 1995.
> From the Tower of London to the Hall of Kings, a look at scary places.

# BIBLIOGRAPHY: ADDITIONAL REFERENCES

*Amazing Animals,* by Philippa Perry. Two-Can Publishing, 1994.

*The Bermuda Triangle,* by Charles Berlitz. Doubleday, 1974.

*Cat Country,* by Di Frances. David & Charles, 1983.

*The Fire Came By,* by John Baxter. Doubleday, 1976.

*Incredible But True!,* by Kevin McFarland. Bell Publishing, 1978

*Lands of Mystery,* by Judith Herbst. Lerner, 2005.

*A Living Dinosaur,* by Roy Makal. Brill, 1987.

*Man and the Stars,* by Duncan Lunan. Souvenir Press, 1974.

*More Strange But True Baseball Stories,* by Howard Liss. Random House, 1983.

*Planet's Most Extreme Eaters.* Blackbirch Press, 2005

*The Probability of the Impossible,* by Thelma Moss. Paladin, 1979.

*Ripley's Believe It or Not.* Scholastic, 2006.

*Sorry, You've Been Duped,* by Melvin Harris. Weidenfield & Nicolson, 1986

*Strange and Unexplained Mysteries of the 20th Century,* by Jenny Randles. Sterling, 1994.

*Strange But True,* by Thomas Slemen. Robinson Publishing, 1998.

*Strange But True Baseball Stories,* by Furman Bisher. Scholastic, 1975.

*Strange But True Football Stories,* by Zander Hollander. Random House, 1967

*Strange Mysteries from Around the World,* by Seymour Simon. Four Winds, 1980.

*Superweird,* by Andrea Urton. Lowell House, 1992.

*Unbelievable But True,* by James Cornell. Scholastic, 1974.

*Weird But True,* by Cindy Barden. Carson-Dellosa Publishing, 2004.

## NEWSPAPER OR MAGAZINE ARTICLES

"Adams Sails the Pacific." *San Diego Chronicle,* July 27, 1969.

"Fish and Frog Rain." *The Athenaeum,* 1841.

"The Pharmacy in the Forest." *Mother Earth News* (June 1995): 40–45.

"Rowers Arrive." *London Times,* August 2, 1986.

"Shower of Frogs." *Scientific American,* July 12, 1873.

"Sure Cures?" *Mother Earth News* (December/January 1995): 46

# Index

# About the Author

NANCY POLETTE is an educator with over 30 years' experience. She has authored more than 150 professional books. She lives and works in Missouri, where she is Professor at Lindenwood College.

DATE

Demco, Inc. 38-293